Taking Children Seriously

A Proposal for a Children's Rights Commissioner

Peter Newell

The first edition of *Taking Children Seriously* was co-authored by Martin Rosenbaum and Peter Newell. This fully revised second edition has been prepared by Peter Newell. Peter is an advocate for and commentator on the human rights of children, in the UK and internationally. In the UK he has chaired the Council of the Children's Rights Development Unit and is Co-ordinator of EPOCH – End Physical Punishment of Children and EPOCH-WORLDWIDE. With Rachel Hodgkin, he co-authored *Effective Government Structures for Children*, published by the Calouste Gulbenkian Foundation, London, in 1996. Peter is an adviser to the European Network of Ombudsmen for Children (established in 1997). For UNICEF he has been involved in advising and supporting the development of independent human rights institutions for children in various countries including Ethiopia, the Russian Federation and the Ukraine.

Sir William Utting

Sir William Utting CB was Chief Inspector, Social Services Inspectorate, Department of Health, before he retired. Among other positions he is a member of the Committee on Standards in Public Life, and President of both the National Institute for Social Work and the Mental Health Foundation. He chaired the independent Commission on Children and Violence which was established by the Gulbenkian Foundation and reported in 1995.

Taking Children Seriously

A Proposal for a Children's Rights Commissioner

New and Fully Revised Edition

Peter Newell

Foreword by Sir William Utting

CALOUSTE GULBENKIAN FOUNDATION, LONDON

Published by the
Calouste Gulbenkian Foundation
United Kingdom Branch
98 Portland Place
London W1N 4ET
Tel: 020 7636 5313

ISBN 0 903319 89 6

British Library Cataloguing-in-Publication Data
A catalogue record for this book is available from the
British Library

Designed by Andrew Shoolbred
Printed by Expression Printers Ltd, IP23 8HH

Distributed by Turnaround Publisher Services Ltd, Unit 3,
Olympia Trading Estate, Coburg Road, Wood Green,
London N22 6TZ. Tel: 020 8829 3000, Fax: 020 8881 5088,
E-mail: orders@turnaround-uk.com

Cover photograph: Maggie Murray/Format.

Contents

Foreword

Ours is an adult society. It runs on rules determined, administered and adjudicated by adults. Adults are not fair even to each other: there is a recognised need for independent commissions to promote equal opportunities and to combat discrimination against minorities. Still less are they consistently fair to children. Public attitudes on matters relating to children veer between extremes, and sharply diverging views are expressed in the media about different groups of children at different times.

These may seem strange statements when so many adults are devoted and sensible parents and governments proclaim their concern for children among other vulnerable sections of the community. Parents, however, are primarily concerned with the welfare and happiness of their own children. This is in itself of inestimable benefit to society, but the influence of parents rarely extends beyond their own children to affect the general social factors which press upon children as a significant group within the population. Governments, moreover, are dominated by the pushes and pulls of an electorate in which only grown-ups have votes, and issues about children are as a result continually overshadowed by the interests of adults. Good results may occur for children in this way, but they are indirect and haphazard.

Many voluntary organisations also provide care, services and advocacy for children. They speak out on behalf of children on specific issues and make common cause on large matters that affect all children. While they may criticise and campaign, however, they do not possess the authority to call other agencies and executive bodies to account. We lack an independent office mandated to protect the interests of children in general on all matters of public policy and administration that affect their lives. Children need a strong, independent, national office to represent their interests comprehensively and to ensure that public and private agencies deliver what law and public policy require.

The case for a Children's Rights Commissioner for the United Kingdom has been stated, modified, redefined and improved during the last decade. Peter Newell's book completes that case and shows how the office would work. Over one hundred voluntary organisations now support the appointment of a Commissioner. The idea of rights for children remains controversial for some people, as if entrenching them in the life of our society would somehow be at the expense of parents. There is the theoretical possibility of conflict if one takes the view that the extension of rights for one group must inevitably be at the expense of the other. Espousing children's rights is unlikely to add materially to the individual cases in which the interests of children come into conflict with those of their parents. The general outcome will be that the rights of children and the rights and responsibilities of parents prove mutually supportive, and that they march hand in hand into the new millennium.

Sir William Utting

List of supporting organisations

The following organisations are among those which support the establishment of independent statutory offices – Children's Rights Commissioners – to monitor, promote and protect the human rights of children in England, Northern Ireland, Scotland and Wales.

Adolescent and Children's Trust
Adoption UK
Advisory Centre for Education
African-Caribbean Family Mediation
    Service
Alliance for Inclusive Education
Anna Freud Centre
Antidote: Campaign for Emotional
    Literacy
Article 12
Article 31 Action Network
Association of Directors of Social
    Services
Association of Lawyers for Children
ATD Fourth World
Barnardo's
BLISS – Baby Life Support Systems
British Agencies for Adoption and
    Fostering
British Association for Early Childhood
    Education
Campaign for State Education
Centre for Citizenship Studies in
    Education, University of Leicester
Centre for Studies on Inclusive
    Education (CSIE)
Child Accident Prevention Trust
Child Poverty Action Group
ChildLine
Children in Scotland
Children in Wales
Children's Rights Alliance for England
Children's Rights Officers and Advocates
Children's Society
Citizenship Foundation
College of Care and Early Education
Community Development Foundation
    (CDF)
Community Service Volunteers (CSV)
Contact a Family

Coram Family
Council for Disabled Children
Council for Education in World
    Citizenship
Daycare Trust
Downs Syndrome Association
EPOCH
Fair Play for Children
Family Planning Association
Family Welfare Association
First Key
Forum on Children and Violence
Gingerbread
Grandparents' Federation
Guides Association
Home-Start UK
Howard League for Penal Reform
International Association for the Child's
    Right to Play – UK Branch
International Play Association
Kids' Clubs Network
Local Government Association
Local Government Information Unit
London Black Women's Health Action
    Project
London Voluntary Service Council
Low Pay Unit
Maternity Alliance
NACRO
National Aids Trust
National Association of Hospital Play
    Staff
National Association for Maternal and
    Child Welfare
National Association of Toy and Leisure
    Libraries
National Asthma Campaign
National Autistic Society
National Childminding Association
National Children's Bureau

National Children's Centre
National Coalition Building Institute
National Confederation of Parent
 Teacher Associations
National Council of Voluntary Child
 Care Organisations
National Early Years Network
National Foster Care Association
National Playbus Association
NCH Action for Children
Network 81
NSPCC
Outset
Oxfam GB
Parenting Education and Support Forum
Professional Association of Nursery
 Nurses
Refugee Legal Centre
Right From the Start
Royal College of Nursing

Royal College of Obstetricians and
 Gynaecologists
Royal College of Paediatricians and
 Child Health
Royal Society for the Prevention of
 Accidents
RPS Rainer
Save the Children Fund
Scope
Scottish Alliance for Children's Rights
Scottish Pre-School Play Association
Standing Committee for Youth Justice
Stonewall
UK Public Health Association
UNICEF (UK)
Union of Muslim Organisations – UK
Voice for the Child in Care
Who Cares? Trust
Woodcraft Folk
Youth Clubs UK

Introduction

As it enters the new millennium, the Government has taken the first momentous steps towards the development of a human rights culture in the United Kingdom. The Human Rights Act 1998 brings the fundamental principles of the European Convention on Human Rights into domestic law. A Committee on Human Rights is to be established in the Westminster Parliament. There is to be a Disability Rights Commission, joining the existing Equal Opportunities Commission and Commission for Racial Equality. In Northern Ireland, a Human Rights Commission is already operating as an integral part of the peace process, and plans for a UK-wide Human Rights Commission remain under consideration. The Scottish Executive is considering whether to establish a separate Human Rights Commission in Scotland.

The Government has termed this process, in the title of its White Paper, *Bringing rights home*. This handbook is about bringing *children's* rights home. Children hold the key to the development of a human rights culture. If children do not enjoy human rights, experience what it means to be a holder of rights and see adults taking their human rights seriously, if human rights are not built into their early development and education and into government and services for them, there can be no serious prospect of developing a human rights culture for our future.

The world has taken decisive steps in a relatively short time span of 50 years towards acceptance of the universality of human rights. Few would dispute that this is the most significant of human developments, the one which provides most hope for a peaceful future, for any future. Internationally, the imperative of respecting children's human rights has achieved remarkably speedy acceptance. In 1990 the largest ever gathering of leaders for the World Summit for Children at the United Nations headquarters in New York committed themselves 'to give high priority to the rights of children'. Within a decade 191 states – all but two of the eligible states worldwide – have ratified the United Nations Convention on the Rights of the Child. The UK Government ratified it with all-party support in 1991. The Convention provides a detailed framework of principles and standards for treatment of the world's children. Unique among human rights instruments, it brings together economic, social and cultural rights with civil and political rights.

It is governments which take on obligations under the United Nations human rights instruments, including the Convention on the Rights of the Child. But the UN system and individual states throughout the world have recognised that making human rights real and ensuring that all enjoy them require the establishment of powerful independent institutions with powers and duties set out in legislation. The UK Government has been particularly prominent in the promotion of national human rights institutions worldwide. There are special, additional justifications for the establishment of independent institutions to promote the human rights of children – in particular the vulnerability of children to adult and government actions, the fact that children have no vote and play no significant part in the political process, and the difficulties for children in using the legal system to protect and promote their rights.

Realising human rights for all is an explicit aim for our Government. The purpose of an independent human rights institution is to contribute to that realisation and to make the Government accountable for its commitment. The distinctive element is independence. A Children's Rights Commissioner is not intended as an agency to fulfil the Government's obligations to children – but to monitor how those obligations are being met for all children and to promote effective implementation; to ensure that children are visible and well placed on the political agenda; that respect for the human rights of all children informs all relevant policy development; that children's views inform policy development which affects them and that society takes children and their views seriously; that children have effective redress when their rights are breached.

Commissioners need to be proactive as well as reactive: for example by proposing and where necessary piloting innovative approaches to the task of implementation. The Government must not be able to dictate or dominate the Commissioner's agenda, but it should be able to call on the Commissioner's help and advice at all times. A close and collaborative relationship between the Commissioner's office and Government is plainly vital. While the overall aims of Government and the aims of the Commissioner for children are hopefully identical, their functions are distinct. The Government cannot fulfil the role of a Children's Rights Commissioner; to state that it is doing so, or that such a post is unnecessary, is to demonstrate misunderstanding of the role, or a worrying degree of complacency.

This handbook sets out in detail the proposal for an independent statutory institution to promote and protect the human rights of children – a Children's Rights Commissioner. Since *Taking Children Seriously* was first published in 1991 the proposal has gained increasing support. There has been advocacy from politicians and from parliamentary bodies: in 1998 the Health Select Committee recommended that 'there should be a Children's Rights Commissioner within the UK... We urge the Government to introduce the necessary legislation to create the office of Commissioner as soon as possible, preferably in the next Session of Parliament.' The Children's Rights Commissioner Bill reproduced in Chapter 4 (page 69) was presented to Parliament as a Ten-minute Rule Bill in July 1999. More than one hundred organisations including three Royal Colleges of Health and the major local government associations support the proposal. There is also evidence of strong public support.

The establishment in 1999 of a Human Rights Commission in Northern Ireland means that in one country of the UK there is already a statutory body committed to the promotion and protection of children's rights alongside those of everyone else, although it is not yet clear to what extent its resources will enable it to focus visibly and effectively on children. In Wales, the new Assembly is committed to establishing a Children's Rights Commissioner, although the limited devolution of powers means it will have to wait for Westminster to accord the Commissioner statutory powers. In Scotland children's organisations, through the Scottish Alliance for Children's Rights, have developed a proposal for a Commissioner for Children at a time when there is a real opportunity for the Scottish Parliament to take this forward. The Scottish Executive is the first governmental office in the UK to announce the establishment of a system of child impact assessment across government. An Office of Children's Rights Commissioner for London has been established with National Lottery Charities Board funding as a three-year demonstration project, coinciding with the new arrangements for a Mayor and Greater London Assembly, to help to make the case for a statutory Commissioner.

The proposal set out in this new edition of *Taking Children Seriously*, while focused primarily on England, aims to contribute information to the debate in all four countries of the UK (and to the similar debates taking place in many countries worldwide, considering how best to establish an independent human rights institution for children). All the UK's 13.2 million children need an independent statutory body to promote and protect their human rights. It is the UK as a whole which ratifies international human rights instruments and thus takes on obligations under international law. A substantial body of legislation, including the Human Rights Act, continues to apply to all UK children. Each of the four countries should have an independent statutory office for children; each office will need the same basic powers and duties as well as links to enable them to work together effectively on UK-wide, trans-national and international issues. But each could have additional and distinctive functions linked to the forms of government and other arrangements for children in each country.

Across Europe, many countries already have independent offices to promote and protect children's rights and in others plans are well advanced. In some (see Chapter 5) there are separate offices for children, children's ombudspeople or commissioners. In others, there is a distinct focus on children's rights within a national human rights institution. The functions set out in this handbook for a Children's Rights Commissioner could be fulfilled by a separate office or within an integrated human rights commission. If a separate office is established, integration with mainstream human rights advocacy is essential. If a Children's Rights Commissioner is appointed within a human rights commission, integration must not mean invisibility and it must be recognised that promotion and protection of children's human rights demands distinct powers and some special characteristics. These considerations are explored in Chapter 3.

Amongst some children's organisations and politicians there has been anguished debate about the use of the word 'rights'. Should we drop it? Would we get further if we were promoting a 'Children's Commissioner'? Such debates are – to use an evocative youthful expression – sad. They miss the whole point of the exercise and do a disservice to children and to all of us: we all need a human rights culture. So we must work together with children to bring children's human rights home.

Background to *Taking Children Seriously*

In 1991 the Calouste Gulbenkian Foundation published *Taking Children Seriously – a Proposal for a Children's Rights Commissioner*. The proposal was widely welcomed by those working with children and young people in voluntary and professional organisations and in local government. In the run-up to the 1992

General Election the Labour Party committed itself to establishing an office of Commissioner as well as a Minister for Children. But the incoming Conservative Government rejected the proposal as unnecessary.

In 1996, the Gulbenkian Foundation published *Effective Government Structures for Children*, the report of a UK-wide inquiry which includes detailed proposals for ensuring that central government is responsive to the needs and rights of children. While focused mostly on the internal workings of government, the report repeats the call for the establishment of a statutory, independent Office of Children's Rights Commissioner, with separate but linked commissioners for England, Wales, Scotland and Northern Ireland. It emphasises that the proposal is entirely complementary to proposals for effective structures within government.

An opinion poll commissioned by the NSPCC to coincide with the publication of *Effective Government Structures for Children* found that overall 85 per cent of respondents supported the establishment of an independent office for children (rising to a staggering 97 per cent of the youngest age-group of 15–24 year-olds).[1]

By the 1997 election, the Labour Party had dropped proposals both for a Minister and for a Commissioner for Children from its manifesto. But a few months after the election the minister responsible for children's services in the Department of Health said that the new Government had not rejected the proposal; there would be an evaluation of existing models around Europe. In 1999 the Government remains unconvinced: 'The Government are not persuaded that it is desirable to create a national mechanism additional to the existing agencies and arrangements for ensuring that safeguards for children are implemented, and their voices heard.'[2] Hence the need for this new edition.

1 The poll was commissioned for the Gulbenkian Foundation Inquiry into Effective Government Structures for Children by the NSPCC. It was carried out by Audience Selection between 29 November and 1 December 1996.

2 Lord Hunt of Kings Heath responding to a question in the House of Lords, 23 February 1999, *Hansard*, col. 949.

Chapter 1

The case for a Children's Rights Commissioner

This chapter places the proposal for establishing an independent office to promote the human rights of children – a Children's Rights Commissioner – in its international and national context.

First, the international context: international pressure to create independent national institutions in every state to promote and protect human rights has grown over the last decade, and the UK Government has contributed to this pressure through its foreign policy. This chapter reviews the background and aims of independent human rights institutions generally.

In relation to children, the almost universal ratification of the UN Convention on the Rights of the Child over the decade since its adoption in 1989 provides the context for ensuring that every state has effective independent institutions to promote and protect *children's* human rights. The Treaty Body for the Convention, the Committee on the Rights of the Child, is strongly promoting the development of independent offices – children's ombudspeople and commissioners – as a key general measure for implementation. The Council of Europe is also promoting this development. There is now a European Network of Ombudsmen for Children and many diverse models of independent human rights institutions for children have been and are being established across Europe and worldwide.

The establishment of Children's Rights Commissioners in the UK is necessary to pursue effectively the obligations under international law which the Government accepted when it voluntarily ratified the Convention in 1991. It fits into the general context of developing independent national human rights institutions which the Government has pursued internationally and has begun to develop on its own territory with the establishment of the Northern Ireland Human Rights Commission. The UK needs to practise energetically at home what it preaches internationally.

Domestically, the proposal should be seen as a central and essential strategy for fulfilling the Government's strongly expressed commitment to develop a human rights culture in the UK.

More generally, the proposal needs to be seen as part of the strategy to make government itself more effective for children and to make children more visible in government by changing its structures and activities. So this chapter ends with a review of where this process has reached and of the Government's current (1999) response to the proposal for a Commissioner. It also reviews existing agencies and services relevant to the promotion and protection of children's human rights.

The overall aims of government for children and the aims of an independent office obviously run parallel. But the key distinctive element of a Children's Rights Commissioner is its independent, human rights-based perspective. It is not intended as an agency to fulfil the Government's obligations to children, but to monitor how those obligations are being met for all children, and where necessary to demonstrate how they should be met. While the Government should not be able to dictate the Commissioner's agenda, it should be able to call on the Commissioner's help and advice at all times. A close and collaborative relationship between the Commissioner's office and Government is plainly vital.

The international context

International pressure to develop national human rights institutions

The development of universal human rights instruments within the United Nations (the Universal Declaration of Human Rights and the two International Covenants, on Civil and Political Rights and on Economic, Social and Cultural Rights) has led to pressure over the last few decades throughout the UN system to create independent national human rights institutions – human rights commissions and ombudspeople. Their purpose is to promote recognition and realisation of human rights at state level. In its foreign policy and through the Commonwealth the UK Government has distinctively contributed to the pressure to establish these institutions and to the provision of technical assistance for their development.

A training handbook from the Geneva-based UN Centre for Human Rights (now the Office of the UN High Commissioner for Human Rights) outlines the development and role of these bodies. When a state ratifies a human rights instrument, it either incorporates its provisions directly into domestic legislation, or undertakes to comply in other ways with the obligations to respect human rights in the instrument.

> Often, however, the fact that a law exists to protect certain rights is not enough if that law does not also provide for all the legal powers and institutions necessary to ensure the effective realisation of those rights… It has therefore become increasingly apparent that the effective enjoyment of human rights calls for the establishment of national infrastructures for their promotion and protection. In recent years many countries have established institutions with the express function of protecting human rights. While the specific tasks of such institutions may vary considerably from country to country, they share a common purpose, and for this reason are referred to collectively as national human rights institutions.

The conclusion to the handbook states:

> There are some who see no good reason for establishing special machinery devoted to the promotion and protection of human rights. They may argue that such bodies are not a wise use of scarce resources and that an independent judiciary and democratically elected parliament are sufficient to ensure that human rights abuses do not occur.
>
> Unfortunately history has taught us differently. An institution which is in some way separated from the responsibilities of executive government and judicial administration is in a position to take a leading role in the field of human rights.

> By maintaining its real and perceived distance from the government of the day, such a body can make a unique contribution to a country's efforts to protect its citizens and to develop a culture respectful of human rights and fundamental freedoms.[1]

Children, unable to exert influence through voting or to play any significant part in our democratically elected Parliament, and unable in general to call on the independent judiciary, are in particular need of an independent human rights institution. And the building of the desired human rights culture for the future is inevitably in the hands of children.

The 1993 World Conference on Human Rights in its Vienna Declaration and Programme of Action reaffirmed:

> ... the important and constructive role played by national institutions for the promotion and protection of human rights, in particular in their advisory capacity to the competent authorities, their role in remedying human rights violations, in the dissemination of human rights information, and education in human rights...

It also encouraged: 'the establishment and strengthening of national institutions'.[2]

The functions of national human rights institutions

In 1993, following a series of workshops and seminars throughout the UN system, the General Assembly endorsed a set of 'Principles Relating to the Status of National Institutions' (see Appendix 2, page 94).[3] The Principles affirm that national institutions are to be vested with competence to promote and protect human rights and given as broad a mandate as possible, 'clearly set forth in a constitutional or legislative text'. Among proposed responsibilities are:

- to submit recommendations, proposals and reports on any matter relating to human rights (including legislative and administrative provisions and any situation of violation of human rights) to the Government, parliament and any other competent body
- to promote conformity of national laws and practices with international human rights standards
- to encourage ratification and implementation of international standards
- to contribute to the reporting procedure under international instruments
- to cooperate with the United Nations, regional institutions and national institutions in other countries
- to assist in formulating and executing human rights teaching and research programmes
- to increase public awareness of human rights through information and education and use of the media.

All of these functions can be re-focused to relate specifically to the promotion and protection of the human rights of children:

- to submit recommendations, proposals and reports on any matter relating to the human rights of children (including legislative and administrative provisions and any situation in which their human rights are violated) to the Government, parliament and any other competent body

- to promote conformity of national laws and practices with the Convention on the Rights of the Child and other international human rights standards relating to children
- to encourage ratification and implementation of international standards which relate to children's human rights
- to contribute to the reporting procedure under the Convention on the Rights of the Child and reporting procedures under other relevant international instruments concerning the human rights of children
- to cooperate with the United Nations and with regional institutions and national institutions in other countries, including in particular national institutions established to promote and protect children's rights
- to assist in formulating and executing teaching and research programmes relating to the human rights of children
- to increase public awareness of children's rights through information, education and the media.

Many countries, in Europe and elsewhere, have developed national human rights institutions. There are two broad and overlapping categories – human rights commissions and ombudsmen. Ombudsmen have traditionally been associated with an emphasis on impartial investigation. The handbook of the Centre for Human Rights, quoted above, suggests:

> Many long-established offices of the ombudsman do not concern themselves directly with human rights except in so far as they relate to their principal function of over-seeing fairness and legality in public administration. Others, particularly the more recently created offices, have been given specific human rights protection mandates, often in relation to the rights set forth in national constitutions or other legislation.

The handbook acknowledges that precise classification of national institutions into categories is impossible, because:

> An 'ombudsman', for example may be engaged in a broad range of promotional and protective activities generally recognised as characteristic of a commission. An entity identified as a 'human rights commission' may be operating exclusively within the sphere of public administration – a domain traditionally associated with the office of the ombudsman.[4]

Children's human rights – an internationally acknowledged priority

The Convention on the Rights of the Child

At the 1990 World Summit for Children, 71 heads of state came together and said: 'The well-being of children requires political action at the highest level. We are determined to take that action. We ourselves make a solemn commitment to give high priority to the rights of children.'[5] And the World Conference on Human Rights in its 1993 Vienna Declaration and Programme of Action reiterated the principle of 'First Call for Children' and stated that 'the rights of the child should be a priority in the United Nations system-wide action on human rights.'[6]

While the UN system has acknowledged that everyone needs powerful independent institutions to promote and protect their human rights, there are obvious additional justifications for children:

- Children's developmental state makes them particularly vulnerable to breaches of their human rights by adults and by governments.
- Children have only recently begun to be recognised as rights-holders, and this still provokes widespread hostility, suspicion and misunderstandings.
- Children have no vote and play no significant part in the political process which determines governments' response to human rights; despite the participation principle in article 12 of the Convention on the Rights of the Child, children's views are not generally respected.
- There are serious problems for children, particularly young children, in using the legal system to assert their rights or seek remedies for breaches of their rights.
- The possibilities for self-advocacy by children, particularly young children, are limited, and generally children in contrast to adults have few organisations of their own.

Human rights are universal, but the world community has underlined the importance of ensuring that children's rights are given special attention by the almost universal acceptance of the Convention on the Rights of the Child. The Convention is a unique instrument covering the whole range of human rights for children – civil and political rights in addition to economic, social and cultural rights. The Convention has been ratified by 191 states, all but two of the eligible states worldwide.

The particular task of the Convention is to emphasise that children too are holders of human rights. They are not possessions of their parents or of the state. They are not simply objects of concern. They are not people-in-the-making. They are individuals *now* with views, feelings and rights. Implementing the Convention is not a favour which it is open to governments to bestow on children. The Convention provides detailed obligations, voluntarily taken on by governments, but then binding under international law.

Article 4 of the Convention requires states to 'undertake all appropriate legislative, administrative, and other measures, for the implementation of the rights recognised in this Convention'. And under article 42, states must 'make the principles and provisions of the Convention widely known, by appropriate and active means, to adults and children alike'.

The Convention requires 'States Parties' – the 191 states which have ratified it – to report regularly (initially within two years of ratification and then every five years) to the Committee on the Rights of the Child. The Committee, established by the Convention, consists of 10 adult experts, elected by States Parties to monitor progress towards implementation.[7]

International surveys show that as states come to terms with their obligation to take the Convention seriously, they find not only that they need new laws and new policies, but that they need new structures and activities to ensure an adequate political priority for children.[8] In 1998 Save the Children published the report of a detailed study, *Implementing children's rights: what can the UK learn from international experience?* The study 'highlights positive ways in which the Convention and the reporting process has been used in other countries as a tool to create dynamic and comprehensive policy initiatives for children at all levels.

In so doing, it aims to inform the development of a coordinated and high-profile agenda for children's rights in the UK.'[9]

Recommendations from the Committee on the Rights of the Child

During the process of examining reports from States Parties the Committee on the Rights of the Child has developed a list of 'general measures of implementation' which it encourages Governments to develop (see box). Amongst them is the establishment of an independent office to promote children's rights.

COMMITTEE ON THE RIGHTS OF THE CHILD
General measures for implementation of the Convention

1 Ensure that all legislation is fully compatible with the Convention.
2 Develop a detailed, comprehensive national strategy or agenda for children, based on the Convention.
3 Develop permanent mechanisms in government to ensure effective coordination, monitoring and evaluation of implementation.
4 Ensure that there is a systematic process of child impact assessment.
5 Carry out adequate budget analysis for children.
6 Ensure sufficient data collection on the state of children.
7 Ensure awareness of children's rights among adults and children and disseminate reports under the Convention.
8 Promote cooperation and coordination with civil society – with professional associations, non-governmental organisations, children and so on.
9 Promote international cooperation in implementation.
10 Develop independent offices to promote children's rights – children's ombudspeople or commissioners for children.

The establishment of some independent human rights offices for children predated the Convention on the Rights of the Child, including Norway's pioneering Ombudsman for Children (in 1981; see page 79). But since the adoption of the Convention in 1989, the development of these institutions is most usefully considered alongside or in the context of the development of national human rights institutions.

The Committee on the Rights of the Child has consistently commended the establishment of independent offices for children. In its guidelines for states preparing their periodic reports under the Convention, the Committee asks for information on 'Any independent body established to promote and protect the rights of the child, such as an Ombudsperson or Commissioner...'[10]

In its comments on Norway's Initial Report, it noted that 'Norway was the first country in the world to establish an ombudsman working for the benefit of children.' It also noted 'the spirit of dialogue existing between the Government, the municipalities and the Ombudsman and civil society including the non-governmental community'. The Committee also commended the creation by the Government of Denmark of the National Council for Children, set up for a trial period in 1994 with a similar role and established permanently in 1997 (see page 83).

The Committee welcomed the establishment of a general ombudsman in Panama but still went on to propose a specific post for children: 'The recent establishment of a "People's Defender" which will monitor the enjoyment of human rights in Panama, including children's rights, is welcomed by the Committee… The Committee recommends that the establishment of an independent body, such as an ombudsperson, be given further consideration by the Government…'

The Committee has stressed in particular the importance of independence from government, for example to China:

> The Committee recommends that the State Party consider the possibility of setting up an independent institution such as an Ombudsperson for children's rights. Such a mechanism can play an important role both in monitoring institutions working in the field of the rights of the child, including in the areas of welfare, education and juvenile justice, as well as in contributing to the more rapid identification of emerging problems in these fields with a view to their constructive solution.

The Committee proposed to New Zealand '… that the office of Commissioner for Children be strengthened and that further consideration be given to measures which would give the office increased independence and make it accountable directly to Parliament'.[11] And when it examined Sweden's second report under the CRC in 1999, it reported:

> While the Committee welcomes the establishment in 1993 of an ombudsman for children, in accordance with the Committee's recommendation, it is concerned about a number of issues raised during the dialogue with the State Party concerning the role, autonomy and structural position of the ombudsman for children. The Committee welcomes the launching of an inquiry into the effectiveness of the ombudsman, carried out by a one-man committee, and encourages the State Party to examine carefully its results and consider reviewing the role and autonomy of the ombudsman for children.[12]

The appointment of independent offices has been strongly promoted also by the Council of Europe, whose 'European Strategy for Children' (1996) proposes the appointment of 'a commissioner (ombudsman) for children or another structure offering guarantees of independence, and the responsibilities required to improve children's lives, and accessible to the public through such means as local offices'. The Strategy puts all its recommendations in the context of the Convention on the Rights of the Child.[13]

Development of children's commissioners and ombudspeople in other countries

Responding to the challenge of the Convention on the Rights of the Child and the more general international pressure to establish national human rights institutions and develop a culture of human rights, many states have established or are establishing independent offices for children (see Chapter 5). The UK Government should be reassured by the evident success and popularity of these offices.

The following is a summary of the general aims of existing independent offices for children – children's ombudspeople and commissioners – in other countries (see further detail in Chapter 5, page 75). Not all offices pursue all these aims (in particular, offices vary according to whether or not they deal with individual cases and complaints from children):

- to promote full implementation of the Convention on the Rights of the Child
- to promote a higher priority for children and a higher visibility of children, in central, regional or local government and in civil society, and to improve public attitudes to children
- to influence law, policy and practice, both by responding to governmental and other proposals and by actively proposing changes
- to promote proper coordination of government for children at all levels
- to promote effective use of financial and other resources for children
- to provide a channel for children's views, and to encourage government and the public to give proper respect to children's views
- to collect and publish data on the situation of children and/or encourage the government to collect and publish adequate data
- to promote awareness of the human rights of children among children and adults
- to conduct investigations and undertake or encourage research
- to review children's access to, and the effectiveness of, all forms of complaints procedures and advocacy systems, for example in institutions and schools, and including children's access to the courts
- to respond to individual problems or complaints from children or those representing children, and where appropriate to initiate or support legal action on behalf of children.

All of these aims are or should be the aims of government too. As noted in the introduction to this chapter, the key distinctive element of these institutions for children is their independent, human rights-based perspective. Their role is to render children and their rights visible, to monitor, cajole, nag, promote and demonstrate innovations and when necessary to criticise, fearlessly but constructively.

The UK context

Making government more effective for children

Over the last 30 years there have been many proposals to create governmental, parliamentary and public bodies in the UK to promote children's interests: an inter-disciplinary Children's Committee, a Minister or Ministry for children, a Cabinet Office Children's Unit, a permanent Cabinet Committee on Children, a House of Commons Select Committee, a Child Welfare Commission, a Children's Ombudsperson, and so on. All these ideas have stemmed from a deep-seated and widespread concern that past and current policy-making and practice in areas which affect children have not given sufficient attention and respect to their rights and interests, and that institutional change is needed to rectify this.

The Gulbenkian Foundation's 1996 Inquiry into 'Effective Government Structures for Children' was a first attempt to look comprehensively at why and how current government structures are failing children and to go on to make detailed proposals. The Inquiry was supported by a broad Advisory Group including MPs from major parties. Questionnaires were sent out very widely and responses received from most government departments, from over 130 organisations and individuals working with or for children and from over 50 governmental bodies.[14]

The report of the Inquiry (see the Executive Summary of the report, Appendix 1, page 86) also summarises the proposal originally published in *Taking Children Seriously* that Government, through Parliament, should establish an Office of Children's Rights Commissioner. It emphasises that establishing an independent Commissioner is complementary to the report's detailed proposals for new structures within government:

> Any government with the political will to adopt the aims highlighted in this report and to implement appropriate governmental structures will see the role of an independent commissioner or commission with statutory powers to be complementary, contributing to the quality of government by assisting and informing, as well as monitoring and potentially criticising government. Just as commissions have been established to promote equality of opportunity and racial equality, a children's commissioner would act as a watchdog. An increasing number of countries have acknowledged the need for such independent offices alongside the need for changing government structures. Once established, children's commissioners quickly become extremely popular with the public.[15]

The proposal for a Children's Rights Commissioner has strong support from organisations working with and for children (see page 8). There is also evidence of widespread public support. An opinion poll commissioned in 1996 found an overwhelming majority of respondents believing that the UK should have an independent office for children, like other European countries. Eighty-five per cent answered 'yes', 13 per cent 'no', 2 per cent 'don't know'. Support was high across all ages and social classes, rising to a staggering 97 per cent of respondents aged 15–24.[16]

The results of consultations with children and young people during 1998–9 have also revealed strong support for establishing an independent institution. One conclusion of research carried out by five young researchers all under 16 years old into young people's concerns and ideas for ensuring that adults listen to them was that children need a high-profile adult to 'stand up for them': 'Have a famous person to stand up for children; have a person that deals with young people and their concerns, that can pass their information onto other adults, so there's a fair point of view from everyone no matter who you are.'[17] A consultation about children's views of the Convention on the Rights of the Child in the UK, commissioned by the Government and carried out by Save the Children in 1999, concluded that there was a clear need to 'establish an office of Commissioner for Children with strategic responsibility for policy and practice development, in light of successful international experience.'[18]

This report does not duplicate the sections in *Effective Government Structures for Children*, based on the widespread Inquiry, which explain and justify why governmental structures need changing. Its purpose is to expand on the particular context and need for an independent statutory office for children – a Children's Rights Commissioner, to propose in more detail how the Commissioner would operate and set out the legislation required to establish the office as an independent body with appropriate powers and duties.

Effective Government Structures for Children was published shortly before the 1997 General Election. In the two and a half years since the election, there has been some tinkering with government for children, some changes and rationalisation in the responsibilities of various government departments for children. There have been welcome individual policy developments for children: the commitment to end child poverty, the Treasury-initiated Cross-departmental Review of Provision for Young Children, Sure Start and the National Child Care Strategy and integrated policies for expanding early years care and education. In response to the cascading series of scandals that have uncovered widespread physical and sexual violence to children in institutions and their homes there have been further inquiries and action: the Quality Protects initiative and proposals to appoint regional 'children's rights officers' responsible for the 200,000 children in all forms of residential care, including boarding schools, and for independent fostering agencies.

In addition, there has been devolution of a variety of powers to the Northern Ireland Assembly, the Scottish Parliament and the Welsh Assembly. There are current moves to develop special government structures and activities for children in these three countries which threaten to leave English children behind in their right to effective and sensitive government (see, for example, plans for 'child-proofing' government policies in Scotland, page 49).

There has as yet been no fundamental change of the kind proposed in *Effective Government Structures for Children* in England, in Whitehall or at Westminster (this report does not attempt to cover in detail the emerging proposals in Northern Ireland, Wales and Scotland). There is no comprehensive governmental strategy for children (although central government encourages local government to develop one through the process of children's services planning). There is no children's unit at the centre of government, although there is now a Women's Unit in the Cabinet Office, and the remit of the Social Exclusion Unit, also in the Cabinet Office, has inevitably led it to focus on some acute forms of exclusion of children. There is no minister in the Cabinet to speak for children and no Cabinet Committee focused on children. There is no real minister for children – merely the perpetuation of a junior ministerial post in the Department of Health with 'children's services' among its many responsibilities; no new coordinating mechanism for children across Government; no new parliamentary focus on children.

Children's views still barely permeate Whitehall or Westminster, but the Government has given support to new organisations for children in care and leaving care, and commissioned some consultation with children in connection with the preparation of the second report under the Convention on the Rights of the Child and under the 'Real Deal' initiative. The Social Exclusion Unit's studies on school exclusions and teenage pregnancy and on 16 to 19 year olds not in education, training or employment also involve consultation with young people.

Children have become a little more visible in government, but the added visibility certainly gives no grounds for complacency. Much of the focus continues to be an unconstructive and unrepresentative one, on 'bad' children, or at best on children as objects of concern. Politicians, aided and abetted by sections of the media, too often persist in demonising children, rather than aiming to value, celebrate, respect and include them. Contrast this with Nelson Mandela's ringing justification for his Government's policy of 'first call' for children: 'Children – at once the most vulnerable citizens in any society, and the greatest of our treasures.'[19]

The state of UK children is nothing less than shocking in a rich industrialised society at the beginning of a new millennium. We should be ashamed of the way we treat children. One in three of our children is living in poverty. While overall health has improved, inequalities in health and in childhood deaths have increased. Death rates amongst children from traffic accidents are the second highest in Europe. Each year over a million children truant from school, over 100,000 are excluded temporarily and around 13,000 permanently. We lock up a high and increasing number of juvenile offenders and the conditions under which some of them are held have been described by the Chief Inspector of Prisons as 'unacceptable in a civilised society', with some children locked up in cells for 22 hours a day.[20]

Forty major children's organisations, responding to the draft second report of the Government under the UN Convention in December 1998 stated:

> The sad fact is that compared with many (probably most) States Parties, both industrialised and developing, there is as yet little sign of a coordinated, strategic approach to implementation and to overall policy development for children in central government. We can only see this – and believe the Committee on the Rights of the Child will see it – as a reflection of a persisting low priority for children in Government, and a lack of visibility for children in Government – despite the various acknowledged positive initiatives which impact on children.[21]

It is hard to see how the Government can dispute the persisting need for more effective structures for government relating to children, emphasised so strongly by those working with and for children. The need for change fits precisely into the aims and the concerns set out in the White Paper *Modernising government* in March 1999: 'Government matters. We all want it to deliver policies, programmes and services that will make us more healthy, more secure and better equipped to tackle the challenges we face. Government should improve the quality of our lives…' To make government both inclusive and integrated, the Paper identifies 'three aims in modernising government':

- to ensure that policy-making is more joined-up and strategic
- to make sure that public service users, not providers, are the focus, by matching services more closely to people's lives
- to deliver public services that are high-quality and efficient.

The White Paper emphasises a commitment 'to be forward-looking in developing policies to deliver outcomes that matter, not simply reacting to short-term pressures'. It barely mentions children, yet without a focus on children that goes beyond short-term reaction to 'problems' there can be no serious hope of achieving the overall aims of *Modernising government.*[22]

Even if government was working consistently well for children, if children had a high political priority and were visible in decision-making and budgeting across government, there would still be a need for an independent office to monitor, promote and protect the human rights of children. There is no sense in which government can fulfil the role of an independent office for children as set out in the following chapters. A Children's Rights Commissioner is not an agent of government. Establishing one would be a positive display of goodwill towards children and an investment in children from a government willing to make itself accountable for its obligations to children. It is also a vital part of the Government's existing commitment to develop a human rights culture.

The UK Government made its first report under the Convention on the Rights of the Child in 1994, and it was examined by the Treaty Body for the Convention, the Committee on the Rights of the Child, in January 1995. When UK Government representatives met the Committee to discuss the report they were pressed about the proposal for a Children's Rights Commissioner. They stated that they were not convinced by the arguments since they felt:

> that States Parties should use and adapt their legal system in order to fulfil their obligations under the Convention. The UK had a wide variety of mechanisms which were playing that role... The creation of a new mechanism might therefore make the situation more confused... The British authorities preferred to avoid creating problems of overlapping responsibilities by establishing a new institution.[23]

The responses displayed a misunderstanding of the role of Commissioner. The Committee's Concluding Observations made clear its view that much needed to be done to respond effectively to the requirements of the Convention. In particular it expressed concern whether 'sufficient consideration has been given to the establishment of mechanisms, including of an independent nature, to coordinate and monitor the implementation of the rights of the child'.[24]

The UK Government's second report to the Committee was delivered and published in August 1999.[25] It makes no response whatsoever to this recommendation of the Committee. While the report generally gives more space than the first report to the views of non-governmental organisations, it does not mention the broad and well-established campaign for a Children's Rights Commissioner. Ironically, in a positive section on the promotion of children's rights in other countries by the Department for International Development (DFID) it refers to 'Establishment and strengthening of effective and appropriate national organisations, within government and civil society, who are concerned with promoting and coordinating implementation of the Convention on the Rights of the Child and with monitoring progress... DFID is currently exploring how best it can support activities in this important area of work.'[26]

Bringing rights home – the Government's commitment to building a human rights culture

The new and strongly expressed commitment of the Government to building a human rights culture should provide the irresistible context for pressing home the case for Children's Rights Commissioners for England, Northern Ireland, Scotland and Wales. In Northern Ireland the UK's first statutory human rights institution, the Human Rights Commission, is already empowered to protect and promote everyone's – including children's – human rights.

In 1998 the Human Rights Act completed its parliamentary passage, incorporating the European Convention on Human Rights into domestic UK law; in the Government's words 'bringing rights home'.

To many commentators' disappointment, the Act does not establish any kind of statutory institution to promote and protect human rights in Britain. In the White Paper which preceded the Bill the Government noted that it had not rejected the proposal to establish a Human Rights Commission. It stated, however, that before a Commission could be established by legislation, more consideration would need to be given to how it would work in relation to existing bodies such as the Commission for Racial Equality and the Equal Opportunities Commission, and in relation to new arrangements to be established for parliamentary and governmental scrutiny of human rights issues:

> This is necessary not only for the purpose of framing the legislation but also to justify the additional public expenditure needed to establish and run a new Commission. A range of organisational issues need more detailed consideration before the legislative and financial case for a new Commission is made and there needs to be a greater degree of consensus on an appropriate model among existing human rights bodies.[27]

Ministerial statements since the Human Rights Act received Royal Assent have left open the question of whether there should be a Human Rights Commission for Britain.

In arguing the case now for Children's Rights Commissioners one must take account of the possibility that a UK-wide Human Rights Commission (HRC) will be established. In Northern Ireland (see box below), where a Commission already exists, the debate has moved on to consider whether children will be better served through the development of a separate office directed solely at the promotion and protection of children's human rights, or by development of such an office within the HRC.

THE NORTHERN IRELAND HUMAN RIGHTS COMMISSION

In Northern Ireland, arising from the peace process and the Good Friday Peace Agreement of April 1998, the Government has established, through section 68 of the Northern Ireland Act 1998, the Northern Ireland Human Rights Commission (the Irish Government similarly committed itself to establish a Human Rights Commission and the legislation has been drafted). While other bodies in the UK, including the Commission for Racial Equality, the Equal Opportunities Commission and the Disability Rights Commission and the various ombudsman offices have functions related to certain human rights, this is the first full-scale human rights institution with statutory powers to be established in the UK (in Northern Ireland it replaces the Standing Advisory Commission on Human Rights). The Commission has general functions which plainly require it to protect and promote children's human rights along with those of adults:

- to keep under review the adequacy and effectiveness in Northern Ireland of law and practice relating to the protection of human rights
- to advise the Secretary of State and the Northern Ireland Assembly of legislative and other measures which ought to be taken to protect human rights
- to advise the Assembly whether a Bill is compatible with human rights
- to promote understanding and awareness of the importance of human rights in Northern Ireland
- to conduct investigations

- to provide assistance to individuals seeking to take proceedings involving law or practice relating to the protection of human rights, and to bring proceedings itself.

The Commission's Mission Statement, issued as it came into existence on 1 March 1999, states:

> The Northern Ireland Human Rights Commission will work vigorously and independently to ensure that the human rights of everyone in Northern Ireland are fully and firmly protected in law, policy and practice. To that end the Commission will measure law, policy and practice in Northern Ireland against internationally accepted rules and principles for the protection of human rights and will exercise to the full the powers conferred upon it to ensure that those rules and principles are promoted, adopted and applied throughout Northern Ireland.
>
> In carrying out its functions the Northern Ireland Human Rights Commission will be independent, fair, open and accessible, while maintaining the confidentiality of information conveyed to it in private. It will perform its functions in a manner which is efficient, informative and in the interests of all the people in Northern Ireland.[28]

Professor Brice Dickson (Professor of Law and head of legal studies at the University of Ulster) was appointed Chief Commissioner, with nine commissioners, one of whom, Patricia Kelly, has been Director of the Children's Law Centre in Belfast since 1997.

The Equality Commission for Northern Ireland has also been established in 1999, amalgamating four previously existing bodies: the Fair Employment Commission for NI; the Equal Opportunities Commission for NI; the Commission for Racial Equality (NI); and the Northern Ireland Disability Council. The Equality Commission will also oversee the equality schemes which all public authorities in Northern Ireland now have to draw up; it will 'proof' these from the point of view of equality based on age, sexual orientation and family status. This process is a development from the previous 'PAFT' Initiative (Northern Ireland Policy Appraisal and Fair Treatment) which attempted to ensure that all levels of decision-making were tested against the principles of anti-discrimination, including discrimination based on age (generally taken in practice to cover discrimination against elderly people rather than children).

Chapter 2 sets out details of the mission, guiding principles and activities of the proposed Children's Rights Commissioners and Chapter 4 the legislation required to establish them. These can apply either to a separate Children's Rights Commissioner or to a Children's Rights Commissioner operating within a Human Rights Commission. The two options and their advantages and disadvantages are discussed in more detail in Chapter 3.

Mapping agencies and services relevant to the promotion of children's human rights

In designing the role of a Children's Rights Commissioner it is essential to map the agencies and services which exist already and are relevant to the promotion of children's human rights in the UK. The following section attempts a brief summary. Once there is a clear commitment to establish Commissioners, the mapping would need to be done in more detail, with adequate consultation with the various bodies involved in the statutory, voluntary and private sectors. This would ensure that the role of a Children's Rights Commissioner is designed in relation to them and does not duplicate functions that are adequately covered already.

In developing our original proposal in *Taking Children Seriously* we examined the constitution and activities of many other independent or semi-independent public offices in the UK which influence the policy of central government, local authorities and other bodies, help individuals obtain redress for grievances, or have similar responsibilities. The offices we looked at included the Commissioners for Local Administration in England, Wales and Scotland, and the Northern Ireland Commissioner for Complaints, the Parliamentary Commissioner for Administration, the Commission for Racial Equality, the Equal Opportunities Commission, the Chief Inspector of Prisons, the Social Services Inspectorate (England), the Official Solicitor's Department, the National Consumer Council, the Council on Tribunals, the Law Commission, the Audit Commission, the National Audit Office, the Data Protection Registrar, the Police Complaints Authority, the Mental Health Act Commission, the Social Security Advisory Committee and the Legal Services Ombudsman.

At the time of writing (September 1999) another new human rights body is in the process of being established: the Disability Rights Commission Act 1999 received Royal Assent on 27 July 1999. The Act establishes a Disability Rights Commission whose duties will be:

- to work towards the elimination of discrimination against disabled persons
- to promote the equalisation of opportunities for disabled persons
- to take such steps as it considers appropriate to encourage good practice in the treatment of disabled persons and
- to keep under review the working of the Disability Discrimination Act 1995 and the Act establishing the Commission.

The Commission will have detailed powers to carry out formal investigations, to issue notices if it believes there is or has been unlawful discrimination and to follow them up.

The Disability Rights Task Force, which includes representation of disabled children's interests, has been considering the functions of the Commission in relation to children, and was due to report late in 1999.

All of the bodies listed above have remits which may touch on the promotion and protection of children's rights (and this is not an exhaustive list). None is directly linked to implementation of the Convention on the Rights of the Child or has children or children's human rights as its prime focus. None reduces the need for an independent body to promote and protect the human rights of children. But a Children's Rights Commissioner, once established, would on occasion need to work closely with all of them.

Some of these bodies were established to promote certain human rights for particular groups, including some groups of children (the Equal Opportunities

Commission, the Commission for Racial Equality and the new Disability Rights Commission). Some are empowered to receive and investigate complaints from children and young people. Some, including the Chief Inspector of Social Services, have a responsibility for inspection of relevant services and for advising ministers on aspects of services for children. Others, like the Audit Commission, have carried out specific investigations into certain services for children. The Chief Inspector of Prisons inspects penal institutions for children and young people and advises on related policy issues.

The report on *Effective Government Structures for Children* contains a detailed review of existing inter-departmental committees or structures relevant to children's issues and also a response from Government Departments – coordinated by the Department of Health – describing current government structures for children (four departments did not respond to the Inquiry: HM Treasury, Department of the Environment, Department of Trade and Industry and Department for National Heritage).[29] These structures are relevant to designing the role of Children's Rights Commissioner, because it will need to relate to all of them and develop a positive and influential relationship with all of them. But again, the existence of a productive focus on children and their rights within some departments, and inter-departmental cooperation in promoting them, does not reduce the need for an independent office.

Government's response to the proposal for a Children's Rights Commissioner

In 1998 the Parliamentary Health Select Committee recommended 'that there should be a Children's Rights Commissioner within the UK... We urge the Government to introduce the necessary legislation to create the office of Commissioner as soon as possible, preferably in the next Session of Parliament.'

The Committee places its recommendation in the context of the failure of Government to produce an annual report on implementation of the Children Act 1989 – a statutory obligation which had been breached in each of the years from 1994:

> This failure on the part of the Department of Health reinforces our view that the time is ripe for the UK to follow the example of a number of other Western countries (including Germany, Spain, the Scandinavian countries and New Zealand) by creating the post of a Children's Rights Commissioner. The UN Committee on the Rights of the Child explicitly recommended the creation of an ombudsman or commissioner in the UK as a means of ensuring that children's rights are promoted more effectively.
>
> Such a commissioner would have the duty of promoting awareness of the rights of children, highlighting ways in which present and proposed policy and practice failed to respect those rights, conducting formal investigations where breaches of children's rights were considered to have taken place (for instance, in cases of abuse in children's homes), seeking to ensure that children had effective means of redress when their rights were disregarded (by, for instance, monitoring children's use of complaints procedures) and carrying out or commissioning research relevant to the safeguarding of children's rights.

The Committee's Report states that the then Parliamentary Under-Secretary of State for Health, Paul Boateng MP, had told the Committee that 'the last Government had opposed the idea of a Children's Rights Commissioner, but the present Government was reopening consideration of the proposal.' He said he personally found aspects of the envisaged role of such a Commissioner 'very attractive'.

The Health Committee also repeats a recommendation made by the same Committee in the previous Parliament that

> there should be a Cabinet Sub-committee on Children and Young People, to ensure that the needs of children – including children looked after – are taken seriously at the heart of Government. We hope that the Government will look afresh at this proposal, particularly in the context of the further proposal in relation to a Children's Rights Commissioner.[30]

In its response to the Health Committee's Report (December 1998) the Government shows sympathy with the overall aim, but not with the specific recommendations:

> The Government agrees that it is desirable to have mechanisms that will keep issues of children's rights and safeguards clearly and firmly on the collective agenda of the Government itself and will ensure that this important dimension continues to be emphasised in the policies of local authorities and all other agencies with responsibilities for children, particularly when they are living away from home.

The response indicated that the Government

> had obtained some information on the 10 or so other countries known to have national Children's Rights Commissioners or posts with similar titles. It is not in the present circumstances persuaded that it would be desirable to create such a national mechanism additional to the role of the courts, the police and the prosecuting authorities, the various Commissions (Parliamentary, Health and local government) which already exist, the responsibilities of local and health authorities to deal with complaints and the various inspection and regulatory arrangements for ensuring that safeguards for children are properly implemented, and that their voices are heard.

The Government response mentions new mechanisms intended to 'durably enable it and other responsible agencies to keep issues of children's rights and safeguards under careful scrutiny'. These are firstly, to ensure a cross-sector children's perspective in the work of the various relevant central service inspectorates (social services, education, prisons, probation and the police) by requiring a periodic joint report from all the inspectorates, every three years or more often if required, dedicated exclusively to children; and secondly, the proposal for Children's Rights Officers in each of the eight Commissions for Care Standards, proposed in the White Paper *Modernising Social Services* for England. The response states that the Government sees these 'two major innovations' as prompted by 'the Government's recognition of the need to strengthen the children's rights and safeguards dimension in the public administration structures through which children's services are provided and regulated. The Government sees them as reflecting its wider obligations under the UN Convention on the Rights of the Child.'[31]

While these are welcome developments which may well help to create better and more coordinated services for children, they are only marginally relevant to the role envisaged for a Children's Rights Commissioner. They relate to specific children and specific services – not to all children and certainly not to the full range of rights covered in the Convention. While they should certainly act in accordance with the UK's human rights obligations, their primary perspective is not one of human rights.

Since 1998 the Government has appeared to be promoting its proposals to appoint regional Children's Rights Officers within the new statutory authorities to be set up to regulate care services for adults and children as a specific alternative to appointing statutory Children's Rights Commissioners. In a House of Commons debate on the Government's White Paper *Modernising Social Services* on 30 November 1998, in response to a question from Llin Golding MP, Frank Dobson, the Secretary of State for Health, said: '… There are arguments for a national children's commissioner and there are arguments for our proposal that it would be better done regionally. On balance we have come down in favour of the regional option.'[32]

But the role of the Children's Rights Officers as set out in the White Paper does not in any sense lessen the need for a Children's Rights Commissioner for England.[33] Their responsibilities relate exclusively to the 200,000 children in various forms of residential care (the large majority in boarding schools) and to independent fostering agencies.

The White Paper proposes a new system for regulating care services for adults and children, creating Commissions for Care Standards (CCSs), independent statutory regional authorities responsible solely for the regulation of care services. These CCSs will have a chair (appointed by the Secretary of State for Health) and management boards including representatives from local authorities and health authorities, plus user and provider representatives. There will be eight for England, based on boundaries of NHS and Social Care regions. Each will have a workforce of inspectors.

In relation to children, the CCSs will be responsible for registering and inspecting all children's homes, residential family centres and independent fostering agencies, and also for welfare inspections of all boarding schools. Within each CCS a nominated high-level officer will take charge of the regulatory function for children, who will be designated 'Children's Rights Officer' for the regional area covered by the CCS (the White Paper rightly highlights the danger of the regulation of children's services being swamped by the very much larger volume of adult services that the CCSs will deal with).

The role of these Officers, 'subject to the CCS itself and to guidance and direction the Secretary of State may issue', will be:

- to help the CCS to give a full and effective coverage of children's services and children's rights in their statutory regulatory responsibilities and in the reports they make on the discharge of their responsibilities
- to ensure that the views of children placed in the facilities and services regulated by the CCS are given proper weight in that regulatory task. This will include close liaison with the new arrangements for promoting the voice of the child in care
- to report directly to the Chief Inspector of the Social Services Inspectorate any significant evidence relevant to the rights and safety of children gained from

the CCSs' regulation and assessment of services for children, which might help local authorities or other providers to improve the services and support they give to children.'[34]

It is clear that the role of these Children's Rights Officers is limited to the functions of the CCSs. In the Care Standards Bill, presented to Parliament early in December 1999, the Officers are designated 'Children's Rights Directors' and the Bill indicates that they 'shall have such functions as may be prescribed'. It is good to see a specific focus on children and their views, and on children's rights, within the new arrangements for regulation and inspection. Experience underlines the importance of providing these particular children with special safeguards. But the role bears no significant relationship to the proposal for statutory Children's Rights Commissioners, which relates to the full range of human rights of all the 13 million children under 18 in the UK.

Parliament and promotion of children's human rights

Parliamentary Select Committees frequently play a vigorous role in investigating issues concerning children. But the existing Select Committees are generally based on departmental sectors such as education, health and social services, and are unable to take a 'joined-up' look at children or the effects of Government on them (although the Health Select Committee in particular has recommended 'joined-up government' for children and the appointment of a Cabinet Sub-committee on children and young people and a Children's Rights Commissioner – see page 29). *Effective Government Structures for Children* proposes that Select Committees with a primary focus on children should be established to promote parliamentary scrutiny of policy and services affecting children (and there have been recent attempts to establish a Select Committee on children and families in the House of Lords). It also proposes that the existing All-Party Parliamentary Group for Children should become more active. In 1998 the All-Party Group commissioned 'child impact statements' on the new Government's Bills (see page 47).

A Parliamentary Committee on Human Rights is to be established following incorporation of the European Human Rights Convention into domestic law through the Human Rights Act 1998. This will provide one parliamentary forum for promoting the human rights of children and effective implementation of the Convention on the Rights of the Child.

A Children's Rights Commissioner would be able to provide evidence to the Committee and encourage a particular focus on children's issues.

Local government promotion of children's human rights

There have been welcome developments within local government which aim to improve coordination of children's services and to promote children's rights. Government guidance on local children's services planning refers to the Convention on the Rights of the Child as providing 'a foundation of values, principles and objectives which can be shared by all the agencies involved in children's services'.[35] Local authorities are required to work together to plan services for children in need (as defined in the Children Act 1989) and many have in fact widened the task towards comprehensive planning for all children. A large number of local authorities and some health authorities have taken a formal decision to adopt the Convention and to use it as a framework for developing and auditing any of their services that affect children (and the local government and health authority associations have cooperated with others in developing guides to this process).[36] Many have developed positive arrangements for promoting children's and young people's democratic participation in local government.[37]

In 1987 Leicestershire County Council Social Services Department established the first children's rights service for looked-after children and young people. Now more than 50 local authorities across England and Wales have children's rights and advocacy services, the majority of which are managed by independent voluntary organisations.

In Oxfordshire in January 1999 a Children's Rights Commissioner was appointed. Funded by Oxfordshire Social Services for an initial period of three years, the Commissioner works in Save the Children's Oxford office and has the support of the county's chief executives of social services, education and health. The purpose of the job is: 'To work with voluntary and statutory agencies to enable them to develop their practice and policy in line with children's rights legislation; to enable children and young people to develop an understanding of children's rights and enable them to participate in local decision-making'. The Commissioner will produce an annual report on children's rights in Oxfordshire.[38]

Children's Rights Officers and Advocates (CROA) is an independent organisation providing support and advice for practitioners working in the field of children's rights and advocacy in various settings. It has published detailed guidance for local authorities on developing children's rights and advocacy services.[39]

These services are vital to the realisation of children's human rights at the local level, and in many cases help children to gain some redress when their rights are breached. They do not reduce in any sense the need for a statutory Children's Rights Commissioner operating at the level of central government and they do not possess any of the powers that a Commissioner would have. A statutory Commissioner would need to develop close relationships with these individuals and services.

Non-governmental organisations (NGOs)

The UK has a wide variety of non-governmental bodies working on behalf of children. Many of them have formally adopted the Convention on the Rights of the Child and many pursue a policy agenda based on the Convention. In 1999 the Children's Rights Alliance for England was formed, bringing together over 100 organisations to work towards the fullest possible implementation of the Convention (similar alliances already exist in Scotland and Wales).[40] A powerful alliance of non-governmental organisations is an essential element in the promotion of human rights, but these organisations have no statutory powers and cannot therefore fulfil the role of a Commissioner. For this reason, these organisations are in the forefront of the campaign for a statutory Children's Rights Commissioner (see list of supporting organisations, page 8).

Independent services, such as the National Youth Advocacy Service (NYAS), Voice for the Child in Care (VCC) and the Independent Panel for Special Education Advice (IPSEA) act for individual children who need support and advocacy – for example helping with problems with the care system or special needs education, or relating to parental separation. The geographical spread of these services remains patchy and they are often over-stretched by the scale of demand. There is a growing call for comprehensive advocacy services for all children. The Children's Rights Commissioner would work closely with such services and encourage their development.

In 1999 a proposal to establish a three-year demonstration Office of Children's Rights Commissioner for London received major funding from the National Lottery Charities Board. An office with a full-time staff of five, and volunteer Commissioners, is to be established (see box below).

OFFICE OF CHILDREN'S RIGHTS COMMISSIONER FOR LONDON

In 1999 a project to establish and operate for three years an innovative, entirely new and high-profile 'Office of Children's Rights Commissioner for London' received sufficient funding to go ahead. The project is timed to coincide with the development of the new strategic authority for London, the Mayor and Greater London Assembly, for which the first elections are due to be held in May 2000. The Office will promote a children's perspective and respect for the views of the child in all aspects of London government. In partnership with others it will seek to develop London as an exemplary child-friendly city.

In particular the Office will promote the involvement of children and young people traditionally socially excluded or marginalised. London's 1.4 million children (defined as everyone from birth to 18) suffer social exclusion and disadvantage to a degree unparalleled in most other parts of the UK.

There is no single body representing the needs and rights of London's children. In many other countries in Europe independent offices – children's ombudspeople and commissioners – have been established to promote children's views and interests and act as a watchdog. While the project is justified as a short-term 'stand-alone' demonstration project to benefit London's children and in particular its socially excluded children, its aim is to influence government and community structures in the long term. During the second half of the project period there will be widespread consultation on how such an Office should be established on a long-term basis.

The Office will have a staff of five and volunteer Commissioners will be recruited – people in the public eye committed to promoting the community involvement of children and young people. The Office is being established as a project of the Children's Rights Development Unit, a registered charity. Major funding comes from the National Lottery Charities Board, with supporting funding from the Gulbenkian Foundation, Bridge House Estates Trust Fund, Children's Society, NSPCC and Save the Children.

Answering arguments against creating a Commissioner

Various arguments have been made against establishing independent statutory offices for children:

- **It would just create an unnecessary level of bureaucracy.**
  The Commissioner would not be a part or a level of government. He or she would operate independently, with clearly defined powers and duties. A key function would be to propose how existing bureaucracies at all levels can work together more effectively for children.

  For Government to suggest it is unnecessary is complacent, and any review of the state of UK children demonstrates that any such complacency is overwhelmingly unjustified.

- **Government has obligations under the Convention on the Rights of the Child – Government should fulfil them itself, not set up an independent office.**
  It is true that the obligations under international law to implement the Convention are the State's. The idea of setting up an independent office is not to create a new agency to carry out the Government's tasks for it but rather to create an independent institution which can consider whether or to what extent the Government's obligations to children are being met, to provide a channel for children's views and where appropriate to act as a powerful voice for children.

- **Money would be better spent directly on services for children, on saving or improving children's lives.**
  This is always a telling argument – especially when so many children in the UK are living impoverished lives and facing unacceptable discrimination in their right to life and optimal development. But establishing a Commissioner would cost little in comparison to the billions of pounds spent at present on negative, 'mopping-up' services for children when things go wrong – child protection, coping with juvenile offenders and their offences, child ill-health, accidents to children and so on. The experience of other countries suggests that an office of Commissioner would be extremely cost-effective, improving law, policies and practice which, in turn, improve the quality of children's lives.

- **Non-governmental organisations can do the job better and are more independent than something set up and funded by government.**
  NGOs are vital but they are not vested with any of the statutory powers and duties proposed for the Commissioner. Even acting collectively, they cannot match the powers of a statutory office.

  It is true that a body established by Government through an Act of Parliament is in some senses not independent, receiving funding from public funds. Independence is seldom absolute (most of the major NGOs in the UK receive quite substantial government funding). The detailed proposals for the office of Commissioner follow the international principles established for national human rights institutions and are designed to maximise independence of appointment and of activities.

- **We already have various human rights bodies: why do we need a special body for children?**

  Children's developmental state, lack of political power and the difficulties for them in using the judicial system justify special attention to the promotion and protection of children's human rights. No existing statutory bodies have a specific focus on children's human rights. As yet it is only in Northern Ireland that the whole population, including children, has a Human Rights Commission.

- **If we set up such a body for children, what about older people, disabled people, women and so on?**

  Everybody needs national independent institutions to promote and protect their human rights. Some other groups already have statutory bodies to challenge discrimination against them, to promote their interests and certain rights: the Equal Opportunities Commission, the Commission for Racial Equality and the new Disability Rights Commission. All other people apart from children have a vote, can take part to a far greater degree than children in the political process and have easier access to the legal system.

- **Most children's interests are looked after adequately by their parents and existing services. If we need a new institution, it should be limited to those children who need it most.**

  Human rights apply to all. There are myriad ways in which current law, policy and practice affects children – some children – adversely. If you look at the full range of rights covered by the Convention, there are very few if any children whose rights are fully realised. If the focus is solely on 'problem' children, on picking up the pieces, it is most unlikely that the Commissioner will be able to make a real contribution to solving problems on a wider scale through encouraging preventative policies. The Commissioner needs to be able to monitor the state of *all* children.

  The purpose of 'joined-up' government for children is to meet the needs of the whole child; setting up a children's rights institution which deals only with some children in some circumstances may well exacerbate rather than alleviate fragmented social policy.

- **Children have needs – not rights.**

  The international community, including the UK Government, has accepted that everyone has human rights. The Government is legally obliged to respect them. We have moved beyond simply extending to children a welfare or charity approach. Of course children have needs, but unless their needs are approached from a rights perspective we are unlikely to make non-discriminatory progress towards satisfying all needs for all children.

1 Centre for Human Rights, *National Human Rights Institutions,* Professional Training Series no. 4 (Geneva, Centre for Human Rights, 1995), paras. 17–19 and 298–9.

2 Vienna Declaration and Programme of Action, World Conference on Human Rights, Vienna, June 1993, UN General Assembly A/CONF.157/23, para. 36.

3 *Principles relating to the status of national institutions,* UN General Assembly resolution 48/134, 20 December 1993, annex (see Appendix 2, page 94 for text).

4 See note 1, para. 44.

5 *World Declaration on the Survival, Protection and Development of Children and Plan of Action for Implementing the World Declaration,* World Summit for Children, United Nations, New York, 30 September 1990.

6 See note 2, paras. 21 and 45 *et seq.*

7 For a full description of the Committee and its role and the reporting process, see the *Implementation Handbook for the Convention on the Rights of the Child* (New York and Geneva, UNICEF, 1998), p. 569 *et seq.*

8 Rachel Hodgkin and Peter Newell, *Effective Government Structures for Children: Report of a Gulbenkian Foundation Inquiry* (London, Calouste Gulbenkian Foundation, 1996), section 6, summarises the results of an independent survey of the development of 'general measures of implementatic n' around the world.

9 Sandy Ruxton, *Implementing children's rights: What can the UK learn from international experience?* (London, Save the Children, 1998).

10 General guidelines regarding the form and contents of periodic reports to be submitted by States Parties under article 44, paragraph 1(b), of the Convention, Committee on the Rights of the Child, CRC/C/58, adopted 11 October 1996, paras. 11–21.

11 See note 7, p. 71; the *Implementation Handbook for the Convention on the Rights of the Child* provides a detailed analysis of the reports and comments of the Committee on the Rights of the Child.

12 Concluding observations of the Committee on the Rights of the Child on the Second Report of Sweden, Report on the 20th Session, Geneva, 11–29 January 1999, CRC/C/84, para.135.

13 Recommendation 1286 on a European Strategy for Children, adopted by the Parliamentary Assembly of the Council of Europe, 24 January 1996.

14 See note 8.

15 See note 8, p. 22 and section 5 p. 101.

16 The survey was carried out by Audience Selection over the period 29 November to 1 December 1996. It was commissioned by the NSPCC for the Gulbenkian Foundation Inquiry into Effective Government Structures for Children.

17 E. Tolley *et al., Young Opinions, Great Ideas* (London, National Children's Bureau, 1998).

18 *We have rights okay: Children's Views of the United Nations Convention on the Rights of the Child* (Leeds, Save the Children England Programme Office, 1999).

19 President Nelson Mandela, in his speech accepting the Nobel Peace Prize, December 1993.

20 See note 8, section 2; also *Growing Up in Britain: Ensuring a healthy future for our children. A study of 0–5 year olds* (London, British Medical Association, 1999).

21 *NGO response to the UK Government's draft second report to the Committee on the Rights of the Child* (London, Children's Rights Office, December 1998).

22 *Modernising government,* Cabinet Office (London, The Stationery Office, March 1999).

23 Record of the examination of the initial report of the UK, 24 January 1995, CRC/C/SR.204.

24 Concluding Observations of the Committee on the Rights of the Child on the initial report of the UK, CRC/C/15/Add. 34, 15 February 1995, para. 8.

25 *Convention on the Rights of the Child, Second Report to the UN Committee on the Rights of the Child by the United Kingdom 1999* (London, The Stationery Office, 1999).

26 See note 25, p. 49.

27 *Rights Brought Home: The Human Rights Bill,* Home Office CM 3782, October 1997, chapter 3.

28 Mission Statement, Northern Ireland Human Rights Commission, Temple Court, 39 North Street, Belfast BT1 1NA.

29 See note 8, p. 55 *et seq.* and Appendix 1.

30 *Children looked after by local authorities,* Select Committee on Health Second Report (London, The Stationery Office, 1 July 1998).

31 *Children looked after by local authorities,*

Government Response to the Second Report of the Health Committee: Session 1997–8, Cm 4175 (London, The Stationery Office), para. 84 *et seq.*

32 House of Commons, *Hansard,* 30 November 1998, col. 546.

33 Department of Health, *Modernising Social Services: Promoting independence, improving protection, raising standards,* Cm 4169 (London, The Stationery Office, 1998).

34 See note 33, paras. 4.41, 4.7 *et seq.*

35 Department of Health, Department for Education and Employment, *Children's Services Planning Guidance,* 1996.

36 Association of Metropolitan Authorities, *Checklist for Children: Local Authorities and the UN Convention on the Rights of the Child,* 1995; British Association for Community Child Health, *Child Health Rights: Implementing the UN Convention on the Rights of the Child – a practitioners' guide,* 1995.

37 Carolyne Willow, *Hear! Hear! Promoting children's and young people's democratic participation in local government* (London, Local Government Information Unit, 1997).

38 Job specification, Children's Rights Commissioner for Oxfordshire, Save the Children, 141–145 Cowley Road, Oxford OX4 1HY.

39 *On the rights track: Guidance for local authorities on developing children's rights and advocacy services,* Children's Rights Officers and Advocates and the Local Government Association, 1998.

40 Children's Rights Alliance for England; for further details contact CRAE, 319 City Road, London EC1V 1LJ, 020 7278 8222.

Chapter 2

The proposal for a Children's Rights Commissioner

This chapter describes in detail the proposed features of an independent statutory office – a Children's Rights Commissioner with staff – to promote the rights of children and young people under 18. The original proposal, published as *Taking Children Seriously* in 1991, was for a UK-wide Commissioner's office, either a single Commissioner with four offices in England, Northern Ireland, Scotland and Wales, or a separate Commissioner for each country with appropriate links between them. Since then devolution has progressed and it seems clear that the way forward is for separate Commissioners, relating to the arrangements for devolved government, but linked to reflect the fact that it is the UK as a whole which ratifies international human rights treaties and takes on obligations under international law. The Human Rights Act and much domestic law which affects children applies throughout the UK. All children in the UK need a powerful independent agency to promote and protect their human rights.

The proposal set out here relates particularly to England, but will hopefully contribute to the advanced and detailed debates on the establishment of a Children's Rights Commissioner taking place in Northern Ireland, Scotland and Wales. These debates underline the case for providing all children in the UK with a powerful statutory office to promote and protect their human rights.

The mission, guiding principles and activities proposed in this chapter for the Children's Rights Commissioner stem in particular from analysing:

- the role and functions of national human rights institutions
- the task of promoting full implementation of the United Nations Convention on the Rights of the Child
- the functions of relevant existing bodies in the UK, to ensure there is no unnecessary duplication of function
- the role and functions of children's ombudspeople and commissioners established in other European states to promote and protect children's rights and the formal evaluations there have been of some of them (see also Chapter 5).

Mission

The 'mission' or fundamental purpose of the Office of Children's Rights Commissioner is to promote the human rights of children. The definition of 'children' is taken from the Convention on the Rights of the Child (article 1) as anyone from birth and under 18. This would be done by:

- influencing policy-makers and practitioners to take greater account of the human rights of children
- promoting compliance with the minimum standards set by the Convention on the Rights of the Child and other relevant international treaties or agreements
- promoting respect for the views of children throughout society
- promoting knowledge of the human rights of children among all children and adults
- seeking to ensure that children have effective means of redress when their rights are violated or disregarded.

Guiding principles

International law

The Commissioner would promote the principles and standards laid down in the Convention on the Rights of the Child (CRC) which should be contained in a schedule to the Act establishing the Commissioner. The Commissioner would encourage the Government and others to comply with the Convention.

The CRC, which was drawn up over a 10-year period, is extensive and detailed. It emphasises that children are holders of human rights. It encompasses civil and political rights as well as economic, social and cultural rights. Recognising children's unique vulnerability and special status it builds for children on the fundamental human rights included in the Universal Declaration of Human Rights and the two International Covenants – on Civil and Political Rights and on Economic, Social and Cultural Rights.

The CRC establishes the Committee on the Rights of the Child as the international Treaty Body, elected by states which have ratified the Convention, to monitor and promote implementation worldwide. The Committee has identified four key general principles among the 42 substantive articles in the Convention:

- non-discrimination: that all rights recognised in the Convention must be realised for all children without discrimination on any ground (article 2)
- best interests: that the best interests of the child must be a primary consideration in all actions concerning children (article 3)
- the right to life and maximum development: ensuring to the maximum degree possible the survival and development of the child (article 6)
- respect for children's views: the right of the child to express views freely in all matters affecting him or her, and to have them given due weight (article 12).

The CRC provides the key statement of principles to guide the Commissioner. This ensures that the Commissioner's actions are founded on a clear body of principles rather than just an individual interpretation of children's rights. The

Commissioner's standing would also benefit from being linked in legislation to a statement of children's rights which forms part of international law. In other countries, legislation establishing children's ombudspeople or commissioners links their powers and duties to the Convention (see Chapter 5, page 75).

The Commissioner would also be guided by other international treaties or agreements signed by the UK which apply specifically to children and young people, or which lay down rights which apply to children as much as to adults. These include the European Convention on Human Rights – now incorporated into domestic law through the Human Rights Act 1998; the Universal Declaration and the International Covenants on Civil and Political Rights and on Economic, Social and Cultural Rights; the Council of Europe Social Charter; and various relevant United Nations rules and regulations – for example those relating to juvenile justice and to equalisation of opportunities for disabled people.

Although the CRC is the most comprehensive document, there are points where other conventions which the UK has accepted provide more detailed or extensive rights for children. The CRC itself states (article 41) that nothing it contains should undermine 'any provisions that are more conducive to the realisation of the rights of the child' which are contained in a state's law or other international agreements in force for that state.

In promoting the rights of children and young people the Commissioner should not be limited to those laid down in international instruments, but would advocate, in the spirit of article 41, further rights that he or she felt were necessary or beneficial in the context of the UK. The international instruments provide a baseline of minimum standards.

There is also a Council of Europe Convention on the Exercise of Children's Rights, passed and opened for signature and ratification in 1996. At the time of writing the UK had not ratified the Convention, which applies primarily to the involvement of children in family proceedings before a judicial authority. A number of commentators have expressed concern that this European Convention falls short of the standards set by the Convention on the Rights of the Child (which all member states of the Council of Europe have ratified), in particular in relation to children's rights to express their views and have them given due consideration. It seems unlikely that this Convention, despite its title, will add anything to the promotion or protection of children's rights in the UK.[1]

Domestic law

Implementation of the Human Rights Act 1998 provides one clear context for the work of the Children's Rights Commissioner. The articles of the European Convention on Human Rights which are incorporated into UK law through the Human Rights Act 1998 apply to everyone, including children. They overlap extensively with the civil rights for children set out in the Convention on the Rights of the Child, but do not cover the full range of children's human rights.

The Commissioner's views on policy would also be guided by some important tenets of domestic law affecting children. For example, the House of Lords in the *Gillick* case decided that children have the right to take decisions for themselves when they have sufficient understanding, except where otherwise laid down by statute (the principle has been eroded by some subsequent judgements, but only in relation to rights to refuse treatment). Another important principle included in the Children Act 1989 (in the context of court proceedings) is that delays in determining questions relating to a child are likely to prejudice the child's welfare and should therefore be avoided.[2] The Children Act was drafted and implemented before ratification of the CRC and while it contains positive principles and provisions in line with the Convention, full implementation of the Convention will demand further development of children's legislation, as it has in all states.

Independence

Although established by the Government through an Act of Parliament and funded largely or completely from public funds, the Commissioner would be independent in action from government and all other bodies, and would be entirely free to determine his or her policy stances and activities within the framework of the law setting out his or her legal powers and duties. The Commissioner's influence and effectiveness will of course depend on using this independence to develop productive relationships with ministers and others.

Width of perspective

The Commissioner would need to keep under review how the responsibilities for children – for the whole child – of many government departments and agencies are exercised. His or her actions would stem from an overall assessment of how policies impact on children and young people. The Commissioner would encourage coordination throughout and between government departments, local authority departments, other public agencies and the voluntary sector.

Working with children and young people

In line with the key principle of article 12 of the Convention, the Commissioner would consistently seek direct contact with children and young people and with organisations of children and young people and direct input into his or her work from them. Children's views should inform every aspect of the Commissioner's work. The Commissioner would promote self-advocacy by children and young people, act when appropriate as a channel for the views of children and as a spokesperson for children or for particular groups of children, thus promoting respect for children's views in government and generally throughout society.

Self-advocacy organisations of children have developed over the last decade. One example is Article 12, a UK-wide organisation of children promoting their rights under the Convention, in particular their article 12 rights, and A National Voice, promoting the rights of children in care and leaving care.[3] As the Committee set up to evaluate the Swedish Office of Children's Ombudsman notes in its 1999 report (see page 81), in order to apply a child perspective, the Ombudsman needs in-depth knowledge of the circumstances of children and the varying needs of different age groups:

> In the Committee's opinion, the Ombudsman should seek knowledge as close to children and young people as possible. This means that the most important source of knowledge must be children and young people themselves, parents, personnel who work with children and young people and organisations that run activities for children and young people.

The Swedish Evaluation Committee emphasises that the task of developing direct contacts with children and young people is so vital that it should be confirmed in legislation (as it is in the case of the laws establishing the Children's Rights Commissioner for the Flemish Community of Belgium and the Danish National Council of Children – see Appendix 3, page 98). A prerequisite for developing contacts with children and young people is that the Ombudsman

> should be allowed greater freedom of action and more opportunities to work flexibly. It is crucial that the Office of Children's Ombudsman has the opportunity to set its own agenda. Contacts with children and young people can never be based on the same structure as cooperation with public agencies and organisations. Such activities require great flexibility within the Ombudsman's own organisation.

Working with other bodies

The Commissioner would cooperate closely and exchange information with organisations working with and for children and young people, in the statutory, voluntary and private sectors. In particular the Commissioner would work closely with regional and local children's rights services and with those providing advocacy to children and young people. The Commissioner should take care to avoid duplicating work already being done effectively by others.

Activities of the Children's Rights Commissioner

The independent nature of the Commissioner's function makes it essential that the office is able to determine its own agenda within the broad aims and duties set out in the legislation establishing it. To pursue its mission the Commissioner would have a range of functions and would need the legal powers necessary to carry them out (see draft Bill in Chapter 4, page 69). The functions include the following: reporting on any area of law, policy or practice affecting children and making recommendations; being consulted by government on proposed new policy; conducting investigations; publishing information and promoting research; reviewing complaints procedures; and initiating or assisting with legal action.

Influencing policy and practice

The overall aim must be to ensure that the human rights of children are adequately considered during all relevant policy formulation and decision-making. This is an obligation of all governments under the Convention on the Rights of the Child. The role of the Commissioner should not be to take over the Government's task, but to ensure that the obligation is fulfilled effectively and built into the process of government. Additionally and whenever necessary the Commissioner can provide an independent view. The following section covers general and specific duties and powers which would form the major part of the Commissioner's role.

Reports, recommendations, etc.

A key part of the Commissioner's role would be to identify and highlight ways in which current and proposed policies or practices fail to respect the rights and interests of children and young people and to suggest measures to rectify this.

The Commissioner would therefore have the general power to examine, report on and issue recommendations on any area of policy or practice affecting children and young people. The Commissioner would be concerned both with policy intentions and with how those policies are implemented in practice.

The Commissioner should not only react to the proposals of others, but also pursue new ideas, in particular ideas that come through direct contact with children and young people. The scope of the Commissioner's work would cover the policies and activities of central government, local government, public agencies, the media, voluntary organisations including especially those working with or for children, and private bodies such as employers or independent schools, as well as European and international developments which affect the UK. He or she could also focus on the relationship between any of these bodies.

The Commissioner must have the right to tackle any issue within any of these fields which he or she feels is of sufficient importance for children and young people. The Commissioner could make recommendations aimed at specific bodies or could issue general guidance. However, since central government sets the parameters within which everyone else operates, government policy would undoubtedly be at the core of the Commissioner's work.

The Commissioner would publish reports with recommendations (as well as an annual report – see below, page 60). They would be circulated to appropriate parliamentary, government, local government and other bodies, and would be available to the public both as hard copy and through the Internet. The Commissioner would need to develop a process for reporting regularly to children (for example, report cards could be circulated through schools). He or she could also issue advisory codes of practice which could first be issued in draft form for consultation with appropriate organisations and with children. Codes of practice could cover, for example, how the principles of the Convention on the Rights of the Child should be put into effect in particular areas of policy or for particular groups of children.

Legislation should ensure that those who are subject to specific recommendations from the Commissioner (including ministers) give them proper consideration. They would have to consider the Commissioner's report and have regard to his or her recommendations. They would also have to respond to the Commissioner within a specified period (say three months unless the Commissioner allows a longer time) stating what action they have taken or intend to take in the light of the recommendations. If they intend not to comply (either partly or wholly) with any of the recommendations they would have to state their reasons publicly. It will be important for the Commissioner to follow up recommendations persistently and devote enough effort to monitoring their implementation, if necessary over quite long periods. The Commissioner would have the right, say, for a five-year period after his or her recommendations were made, to require reports on progress towards their implementation.

In some circumstances the Commissioner may conclude that particular provisions within the Convention on the Rights of the Child as ratified by the UK are not being complied with by a particular body or bodies. In this case the Commissioner could issue a 'compliance notice' which would give details of the failure and state how in the Commissioner's opinion it should be remedied. The new Disability Rights Commission has the power to issue 'non-discrimination notices' when it finds unlawful discrimination and to follow them up.[4] The law on responding to the Commissioner's recommendations would also apply to compliance notices. In these cases the Commissioner could also be given the power, where the body involved still fails to comply, to have this fact publicised (e.g. in national or local newspapers) at the body's expense – this is similar to the extended powers of the Commissioners for Local Administration and those of the Legal Services Ombudsman. The Commissioner could maintain a public register of compliance notices.

As an independent office the Commissioner would not be part of the decision-making apparatus of the Government or of any other body and could not therefore have direct control over any area of policy and decisions concerning children and young people. This independence is essential if the Commissioner is to undertake, and be seen by others to undertake, a disinterested scrutiny of all aspects of the government's and other bodies' policy and activity affecting children.

Constitutionally decisions within the responsibilities of central and local government must in the end be taken by elected ministers or councillors who are accountable to voters. They should not be overridden by unelected officials (although of course the courts may intervene if those elected act against their legal duties or outside their legal powers). Therefore fundamental constitutional principles require that the Commissioner's policy recommendations cannot be binding on the elected bodies concerned.

In any case the introduction of binding recommendations from the Commissioner would almost certainly lead to an appeals process and legal actions from bodies reluctant to comply. This would be time-consuming and would increase the staffing and budget (especially for legal cases) required by the Commissioner's office. In these cases the implementation of the recommendations would also be subject to delays and the risk of being overturned. Organisations may also be less cooperative and open with the Commissioner in discussing policy if they think that later on they are going to be doing battle in court. Neither the Commission for Local Administration in England, Wales and Scotland, nor the Health Service Commissioner, for example, can issue binding recommendations. Of course legal action could be instituted in circumstances where it was found that the law was being broken.

It is essential that the Commissioner is not primarily reactive but is free to choose the areas he or she reports on and can act on his or her own initiative in the light of his or her own priorities. The Commissioner will only be able to work on a limited range of issues at a time. It will be essential to consider carefully what the priorities should be. The criteria used to define priority issues could include the following: the number of children and young people affected; the seriousness of the way in which they are affected; whether those affected are also disadvantaged in other ways; the extent to which the issue has been raised already or is being raised effectively by others; the likelihood of achieving positive change; and the possible 'knock-on' effects for other situations.

Some of the Commissioner's time would be spent on responding to requests for his or her views from other bodies, whether in response to specific invitations or as a part of normal open consultative exercises. The Commissioner could be asked by ministers to examine and report on particular areas of policy, and would normally comply (and below it is suggested that the Commissioner should be required to comment on particularly relevant legislative proposals). However, since a wide range of government departments have responsibility for children's matters, the Commissioner could receive requests from a number of different departments and it would need to be within the Commissioner's discretion to decline. In order to maintain independence it is essential that the Commissioner can set his or her own agenda, and not have it swamped by Government (see, for example, the 1999 comments of the Committee which evaluated the Swedish Children's Ombudsman, Chapter 5, page 81).

Influencing proposed new government policy: requirements to consult the Commissioner

It is better to influence policy while it is being conceived rather than after it has been put into practice. One way to seek to ensure that new legislation or central government policies take into account the rights and interests of children and young people would be for the department involved to consult the Commissioner at an early stage (and certainly before instructions are given to Parliamentary Counsel, who draft government Bills). The Commissioner would analyse and comment on proposed new policies in terms of their likely impact on children and young people. This process would be informed by children and young people themselves. We would expect that on the basis of its expertise the Commissioner's office would build up close informal links with civil servants in all relevant government departments.

Whenever ministers intend to amend or repeal specified major pieces of legislation affecting children they should be required to consult the Commissioner at an early stage. The Commissioner would then have a duty to consider and respond to the points raised. This would apply, for example, to the Children Act 1989, major Education Acts, Adoption Acts, the Children and Young Persons Act 1933 and other legislation relating to offences against children, child protection and offences by children. A full list of such Acts could be spelt out in an order issued under the Act and this could be added to by further orders. This consultation requirement would also be included in appropriate Acts passed in future. A similar requirement would apply to the making or repealing of statutory instruments under specified sections of specified Acts. The Commissioner could issue a dispensation from the requirement to consult in the case of changes which are technical or unimportant. (The requirement on ministers to consult the Commissioner should also apply when the Government considers how to respond to private members' legislation attempting to alter the specified Acts.)

Each government department should also have a Code of Consultation containing advice to consult the Commissioner at an early stage on any proposals which could impact particularly on children or affect children differently from the way adults would be affected. The Code could also require that departments should inform the Commissioner when they start work on a relevant new issue. The text of the Code and the criteria for triggering consultation would be agreed between the Commissioner and each department, or possibly one Code would be agreed between the Commissioner and the lead department relating to him or her and be circulated to other departments. The extent of the Commissioner's ability to comment would have to depend on his or her resources at the time.

Child impact assessment

The first edition of *Taking Children Seriously* suggested that the Commissioner should have the power to require government departments to issue a 'child impact statement' to accompany White Papers, Green Papers, Bills etc., to indicate the likely impact on children and young people.

Since 1991 there has been much debate and – in Scotland at least – some Government action on developing this concept of child impact assessment.[5]

The overall aim must be that child impact assessment is built into the process of government, from the earliest stage of policy formulation, through the development of formal proposals and legislation. And implementation of policies and laws should include an ongoing process of child impact evaluation. As a report published by the All Party Parliamentary Group for Children in 1999 states, for child impact assessment to become an integral part of government itself it would need support at the highest level of government, i.e. from the Cabinet and Prime Minister: 'Without this support a government-based experiment in child impact statements would be unlikely to succeed in its key objective of making children and their rights visible across government.' The report also suggests that 'the process will only work consistently and effectively if some person or body has charge of them... The point is that child impact statements must be the responsibility of a body sufficiently politically powerful to have influence in Cabinet and some leverage over the large functional departments.' It goes on to propose that there are at least three viable possibilities:

- First, child impact statements could be required by legislation to be the responsibility of a Minister for Children or a Children's Unit sited in the Cabinet Office or near the heart of government.
- Second, a Children's Rights Commissioner could be empowered by statute to commission child impact statements and follow them up.
- Third, a Parliamentary Select Committee for Children could be given powers and obligations to commission and consider child impact statements.

None of these bodies exists as yet. The report raises the question which of these bodies would be preferable:

The answer is that, ideally, all three should be involved in a child impact study – a Minister or Unit to secure that the civil service undertakes child impact analysis on a routine basis, a Commissioner to act as an external watchdog on this process and to organise independent assessments when this is thought to be needed, and a Parliamentary body to receive the information during the passage of legislation and to hold the Government accountable to its actions on behalf of children (for example through Parliament recommending the appointment of special standing committees or special 'hearings', or by annual appraisals of a report on children to Parliament by the Government).

The report suggests that child impact

must be built into the internal working of government, within and across government departments. Generally, child impact assessment needs to be part of:
- the development of policy from the earliest possible stage
- any Parliamentary or other formal consideration of its adoption and

- the follow-up monitoring and evaluation (during and after implementation).
So, ideally, one is talking about a process of continuous assessment and more than one child impact statement.[6]

It seems clear that the extent of the Commissioner's role in child impact assessment must depend on the extent to which Government takes the process seriously. On the other hand, however comprehensive the Government's response, there will be a need for an authoritative independent element in the process. This report therefore repeats the proposal in *Taking Children Seriously* that the Commissioner should have the power to require government departments to publish a 'child impact statement' to accompany White Papers, Green Papers, Bills and so on. But in proposing this it should be recognised that the power may need some amendment in relation to the role of government in child impact assessment which may develop in England, Northern Ireland, and Wales – and is already developing in Scotland (1999).

The Commissioner could also request a child impact statement on, for example, the Budget and other statements on public spending. (It would of course be unrealistic to expect the Chancellor to consult the Commissioner on a Budget prior to the Budget speech, but this would be a way of applying a children's perspective to one of the government's most important annual events.)

A blanket requirement to issue child impact statements on all policy proposals would probably be treated as a formality to be observed in a minimal way and would thus devalue the concept. On the other hand the 1997–8 experiment, described in the All Party Parliamentary Group for Children report, assessing the child impact of 23 Government Bills (almost the whole body of government legislation for the period) demonstrates that 'very few policies and Bills have no impact on children'. The report concludes from the experience of commissioning the 23 statements that 'a small amount of research will quickly reveal which policy measures will most profit from a child impact statement – relatively brief conversations with the responsible civil servants and with organisations representing affected interests would be enough to determine when it would be useful to order an impact statement.'[7]

Child impact assessment is perhaps most needed for measures which are not designed specifically with children in mind, as well as for those which impact on both children and adults, and where the impact on children may not receive sufficient attention. The process of requiring child impact statements could also help promote coordination between different departments since any statements they issue would be compared. Giving the Commissioner the power to require child impact assessment would also encourage departments to ensure that they consult the Commissioner properly at the earliest possible stages of policy development. Departments would be obliged to respond to comments the Commissioner made on a child impact statement.

Aside from statutory requirements for consultation on changes to specified Acts, the procedures laid down in a Code of Consultation, and the child impact statement process, the Commissioner could also comment to ministers on Bills, White Papers, Green Papers, and other proposals, formally and informally.

The passing of the Human Rights Act 1998 provides ministers for the first time with a statutory requirement to consider the implications of new legislation for human rights, or at least for the basic civil and political rights in the European

Convention on Human Rights which are incorporated into domestic legislation by the Act. These human rights apply to children as to everyone else. The minister in charge of a Bill in either House of Parliament has to make a written statement of compatibility with the 'Convention rights' (those rights which are incorporated by the Act), either saying that in the minister's view the provisions of the Bill are compatible, or that he or she cannot make such a statement but nevertheless wishes Parliament to proceed with the Bill (section 19). The Commissioner could, when necessary, provide a comment on the compatibility of the Bill with children's human rights, and should in any case be consulted before the Bill is presented.

Beyond this there is as yet no obligation whatsoever in domestic law to consider the impact of new policy or legislation on the human rights of children.

In Scotland, the Minister for Children's Issues produced a 'Scottish Office Child Strategy Statement' in 1998, aiming to ensure that all departments of the Scottish Office explicitly considered the impact of all policies on children before they were implemented. When the Scottish Parliament was formed in 1999, the same Minister – Sam Galbraith – became Minister for Children and Education and a Children's and Young People's Group was formed within the Scottish Executive Education Department. The Group is now (autumn 1999) responsible for determining how these issues will be pursued under the new arrangements for Scottish government.

The Child Strategy Statement encourages departments to ask themselves the following questions:

- Does the policy have any direct implications for children and if so, what are they? How can the policy positively enhance opportunities for children in Scotland?
- Does the policy have an indirect effect of any significance on children, e.g. changes to traffic law which might have beneficial or adverse effects on children's road safety?
- What impact will the policy have on the general welfare of children, e.g. changes to homelessness legislation which might affect children in a number of ways?
- Will the policy affect one group of children more than others, or will there be competing interests between different groups of children?
- Will the policy positively or adversely affect other policy areas, local authorities, voluntary organisations or others in their work with children, and is there scope for integrating the new policy with other measures in train or in prospect?

Following consideration of these questions, departments should consider whether there is a need for consultation, including consultation direct with children, and what else needs to be done to implement the Child Strategy effectively.

The Scottish Executive is committed to consultation with children and young people; in autumn 1999 it was consulting with them on the first major Bill to go before the Scottish Parliament, the Improvement in Scottish Education Bill. The Executive has also endorsed the formation of a Scottish Youth Parliament for young people aged between 14 and 25.

In some other European countries – notably in the Flemish community in Belgium, and in Sweden – there have been developments to require government to carry out child impact assessment. The Flemish Parliament adopted a decree in 1997 which requires that government policy shall be monitored in relation to the provisions of the Convention on the Rights of the Child: 'All proposed decrees when laid before the Flemish Parliament shall be accompanied by a report on their impact on children, to the extent that the proposed decision directly affects the rights of the child.' The Flemish Government can derogate from the requirement to provide an impact assessment following advice from an expert commission which it appoints (and the decree allows for staged implementation of the process, to cover all government departments within five years). The report may be drafted by civil servants, or through a contract with 'one or more centres specialised in the production of such reports'.

The Flemish legislation requires that impact reports must include at least:

- the impact of the proposed decision on children
- the alternatives to the proposed decision, and in particular a description of the measures to be taken to avoid or to limit significant damaging effects of the decision, and if possible to remedy them
- a list of the difficulties encountered in the collection of the required information.[8]

In Sweden, the Parliament adopted a Bill in March 1999 proposing a strategy for implementation of the Convention, including arrangements for child impact analysis at central and local government levels. An explanatory fact sheet from the Ministry of Health and Social Affairs states that there must be a systematic attempt to make the child perspective more visible in decision-making:

> An analysis of the impact of decisions which clearly affect children's lives should be made in each individual case. This should apply to budgetary decisions, legislation and decisions relating to the physical environment. The Swedish National Audit Office, in consultation with the Children's Ombudsman, will be commissioned to draft guidelines for how such analyses might be carried out.[9]

Investigations

Like other similar statutory bodies – the Equal Opportunities Commission (EOC), Commission for Racial Equality (CRE) and the new Disability Rights Commission – the Commissioner would need wide formal powers to launch investigations in furtherance of his or her duties, including powers to gain access to records and documents, to enter institutions and also to question individuals. The ability to launch formal investigations would ensure that the Commissioner had access to objective evidence which might be needed to discover and demonstrate denials of the rights and interests of children. Investigations could be held into the policy and practice of one body or institution or of a number of connected or similar bodies. The Commissioner would be required to give proper notice of the investigation and its purpose to those concerned, and where appropriate there would be guarantees of confidentiality for information supplied. A report containing any recommendations for action would be issued after any investigation.

The Commissioner would need to consult with other bodies with investigatory powers or responsibilities such as the Commissioners for Local Administration, the Social Services Inspectorate, the Chief Inspector of Prisons, the CRE, the EOC and the Disability Rights Commission to ensure that overlapping or conflicting investigations are avoided. (Joint investigations into issues of mutual concern could be considered but might be difficult because of the different legal requirements governing the various organisations' powers to hold investigations.)

Particular functions given to similar independent offices in other countries include in some cases a role in child abuse and child death investigations. In New Zealand the Commissioner for Children supervises case reviews following the death of, or a serious incident involving, any child who is the responsibility of the state. In Australia, ombudsmen for children have been established in Queensland and New South Wales as a direct result of official inquiries into paedophile activities. In New South Wales legislation passed in 1999 gave the general ombudsman's office certain duties and powers related to child protection investigations and convictions of people working in institutions for the care and/or education of children in the state and private sector.[10]

In the UK over the last two decades there has been a continuing series of scandals involving physical and/or sexual abuse of children in institutions, in various other forms of care and within families. In many cases independent inquiries, including judicial inquiries, have been established at huge expense. It is possible that the office of Commissioner could be given specific powers and duties to enable it to oversee, carry out or commission such inquiries. This could be cost-effective; it could also provide such inquiries with a consistent perspective (rooted in the UN Convention) and a cumulative and direct input into policy development. Unlike one-off inquiries, the Commissioner's office would be there to follow recommendations and action through and provide continuous assessment of their effectiveness.

It is not proposed that the Commissioner should have a general role of responding to individual cases and complaints (see below, page 55). But the power to launch investigations would enable a particular case or issue to be taken up in exceptional circumstances, when other responses have proved inadequate, or because of its particular relevance to the promotion of children's human rights.

Information and research

The Commissioner would be able:

- to publish and distribute information about children's human rights (but would avoid duplicating material already published by others)
- to conduct or commission research. The Commissioner would rarely if at all conduct original field research, given the range of bodies already involved in research concerning children and young people, but he or she might want to conduct or commission applied research closely linked to the development of policies and in particular to ascertain children's views
- to review the government's collection of statistics concerning children and

young people and report on gaps, inadequacies and possible improvements (but the Commissioner would not be directly involved in collecting statistics). This would be a useful exercise because attention has often been drawn to the need for more comprehensive and consistent sets of statistics about children in the UK.[11]

The Commissioner would have a particular duty related to the Government's obligation under the Convention to make its principles and provisions known to adults and children alike 'by appropriate and active means' (article 42). The Government has as yet (1999) done very little to fulfil its obligation under this article. The Committee on the Rights of the Child, in its comments on the Government's first report under the Convention on the Rights of the Child, recommended that:

> in line with the provisions of article 42 of the Convention, the State Party should undertake measures to make the provisions and principles of the Convention widely known to adults and children alike. It is also suggested that teaching about children's rights should be incorporated into the training curricula of professionals working with or for children, such as teachers, the police, judges, social workers, health workers and personnel in care and detention institutions.[12]

The Committee's guidelines for states on preparing periodic reports under the Convention seek detailed information on measures taken to implement article 42, including in schools, in parenting education and through training of those working with and for children.[13]

The Committee has underlined the importance of disseminating the Convention's principles and provisions to all sectors of the population. It has suggested that a 'comprehensive strategy' and 'systematic and continuous steps' are needed. In addition, it has suggested that the Convention should be incorporated into school curricula and into the training of those who work with or for children.

There has been some limited research demonstrating a high level of ignorance amongst children in the UK about human rights standards. A study of *School based understanding of human rights in four countries*, published by the Department for International Development in 1998, included interviews with children aged 14–16 in Northern Ireland. One of the questions they and children in three developing countries were asked was whether they had been told in school about the rights in the Convention on the Rights of the Child. Just 6 per cent of the children in Northern Ireland said that they had, compared with 43.5 per cent in Botswana, 53 per cent in Zimbabwe and 68 per cent in India.[14]

A central aim must be to promote a culture in which the human rights of children are understood and respected. Currently, there is much misunderstanding about the nature and implications of their rights.

In 1997 the Government established the Citizenship Advisory Group, chaired by Sir Bernard Crick. Its remit was to provide advice on effective education for citizenship in schools. The Group's report, which was published in September 1998, recommended that citizenship education should be a statutory entitlement in the curriculum and that children should be taught about human rights including the UN Convention on the Rights of the Child and the European Convention on Human Rights.[15] It is hoped that subsequent revisions to the curriculum and guidance will follow this recommendation.

The Human Rights Task Force, established by the Home Secretary to help government departments and other public authorities with implementation of the Human Rights Act, has an additional aim, to 'increase general awareness, especially among young people, of the rights and responsibilities flowing from the incorporation of the European Convention on Human Rights and thus to help build a human rights culture in the United Kingdom'.

The Commissioner's task would not be to fulfil the Government's obligations under the CRC, but to monitor implementation and to propose ways of fulfilling the obligation effectively.

Complaints

While this report does not advocate giving the Commissioner the role of investigating individual complaints from children, an important task would be to seek to ensure that children and young people have effective means of redress when their rights are disregarded.

This is a necessary part of the Commissioner's role of promoting policies which protect children's rights. In relation to any body which has responsibilities affecting children and young people there need to be adequate processes for dealing with cases where the rights of individuals may have been infringed. The Commissioner would monitor complaints procedures to see that they are operating properly and in all relevant fields. And of course the Commissioner's wider work should have the effect of empowering children and young people and reducing infringements of their rights in the first place.

Reviewing complaints procedures

Children have access to various complaints procedures in relation to some of the services provided for them. Implementation of the Children Act 1989 required local authorities to establish procedures to consider 'representations including any complaints' from children they are looking after and any other children who are 'in need' (section 26). The Act's definition of 'in need' includes children who are unlikely to achieve or maintain a reasonable standard of health or development, or whose health or development is likely to be significantly impaired without local authority help, as well as those who are 'disabled' (section 17). There are serious concerns about the degree of independence of these complaints procedures. A new NHS complaints procedure was introduced in 1996, and the Health Service Commissioner for England is able to consider complaints which have not been satisfactorily resolved through the NHS procedure (since 1996 the Commissioner has been able to look into complaints about family health service practitioners such as family doctors and dentists).

There are also the Commissioners for Local Administration (see below, page 55) and complaints procedures provided by various statutory, voluntary, private and professional bodies. (In addition to an appendix in *Taking Children Seriously*, another Gulbenkian Foundation report, *One scandal too many*, provided a detailed review of existing complaints procedures in 1993).[16] However, there remain serious inadequacies and gaps in existing procedures from a children's perspective. Furthermore it is clear from the research for *Taking Children Seriously* and for this and other reports that the use by children and young people of existing procedures is very limited – unsurprising given how little attention has been paid in most cases to ensuring that they are accessible and well-publicised to children.

An important task for the Commissioner would be to review the full range of services used by children and young people, and existing complaints procedures available to them, in order to reveal gaps and inadequacies. The Commissioner would rely in particular on the views of children and young people. He or she would need to work closely with organisations of children like Article 12 and A National Voice (see page 42) as well as with the various inspectorates for children's services, with the regional 'Children's Rights Officers' responsible for regulation of children's residential care, with local authority-based children's rights officers and services and with non-governmental children's organisations. In particular the Commissioner would wish to ensure that complaints procedures are comprehensive, designed for children and easy for them to use, well-publicised, speedy and effective. The Commissioner could collaborate with children and others in drafting a code of good practice for complaints procedures.

The Commissioner would have the power to receive information about and report on complaints made by children or those acting on their behalf to the full range of statutory complaints procedures, and on their outcomes. The Commissioner would not be able to review individual decisions on complaints. While it may not be possible to require those running complaints procedures and advocacy and advice services for children in the voluntary and private sectors to provide the Commissioner with similar information, it should be possible to negotiate voluntary agreements. The rights of individuals to confidentiality would of course be respected.

Having access to this information would enable the Commissioner to assess how complaints are handled and whether their outcomes are satisfactory. Legislation governing any statutory complaints procedures should be amended to ensure that those running them have a duty to 'have regard to' advice provided by the Commissioner. The information would also provide the Commissioner with invaluable data on the concerns of children and young people which would be useful in commenting on law, policy and practice in the wider role of promoting children's human rights.

It is clear that some extensions to statutory complaints procedures are necessary. For example, it is likely that the Commissioner would press for the following:

- extending the powers of the Commissioners for Local Administration, e.g. to cover internal school matters and to allow them to initiate an investigation without having received a complaint (the Local Commissioners have themselves pressed for these changes).
- extending the remit of the Mental Health Act Commission to cover 'informal' patients. Most children in mental hospitals are informal patients admitted by their parents, and only the few detained under the Mental Health Act come under the Commission (the Commission has itself sought this change; the Mental Welfare Commission for Scotland has a much wider remit).

- requiring local education authorities (and governing bodies of grant-maintained schools and proprietors of independent schools and non-maintained special schools) to set up comprehensive complaints procedures for pupils including an independent element. At present local education authorities need only have procedures for complaints about the curriculum and religious worship in schools.[17]

The Commissioner should be consulted by ministers and other relevant bodies on the creation of any new complaints procedures which could be used by children and young people.

Individual complaints

Taking Children Seriously suggested that it would be unrealistic and unhelpful to children and young people and wasteful of resources to give the Commissioners the role of investigating individual complaints from the UK's 13.2 million children and young people under 18. To try to fulfil this role without large resources and a substantial network of local offices and advocacy schemes would mean offering children a remote and inaccessible centralised system. It is clear that children are unlikely to use procedures that are not local and readily accessible. Such a service might also duplicate or conflict with the procedures and sources of help already available to children and young people. If these are regarded as unsatisfactory by children and young people and by those working with them they should be improved, and the Commissioner could play a key role in that process.

At a later stage it may be possible, if the resources are available and if it seems necessary in the light of the Commissioner's experience, to add to his or her role – or create separately – a carefully designed local system to receive and investigate children's complaints across a defined range of services.

Alternatively, the Commissioner could be given the role, acknowledged in legislation, of investigating cases where existing 'lower-level' complaints procedures have failed to resolve the issue satisfactorily. In exceptional cases the wide powers proposed for the Commissioner to initiate investigations (see above, page 50) would enable him or her to investigate an individual case. In general it is envisaged that this would be limited to cases which raise important questions of principle which the Commissioner cannot tackle in other ways. Another possibility which could be examined is that the Commissioner should be able to refer particular cases to the Commissioners for Local Administration for investigation, when there is no other appropriate procedure, even where they fall outside the Local Commissioners' current remit.

There are currently three Local Government Ombudsmen (LGOs) for England, one for Scotland and one for Wales. Any member of the public, including children, may complain to the LGO that he or she has suffered an injustice because of maladministration by a local authority or some other local body. The LGOs have the powers of the High Court to obtain written or oral evidence from anyone. In order to conduct an investigation they have to receive a specific complaint and certain matters (including the conduct, curriculum, internal organisation, management or discipline of any school) are excluded from their jurisdiction. The three English LGOs received 14,969 complaints during the year ended

31 March 1998. These are not analysed by age of complainant. Children may complain direct and the LGO is not required to obtain the consent of the parent or guardian before investigating. Where a parent complains on behalf of a child, the LGO 'would normally confirm that the child wished to have the complaint made on his or her behalf'. It is clear that very few complaints have been submitted by children to the LGOs for England, Wales and Scotland.

The very much smaller child populations of Northern Ireland (491,000), Wales (707,000) and Scotland (1,216,000) compared with England (11,724,000) suggest that in the first three countries a Children's Rights Commissioner with a local network of offices could have a realistic role in the consideration of individual complaints. But the issue of local access and the relationship of the Children's Rights Commissioner's complaints procedures to the LGOs and to procedures already set up for particular services and groups of children would still need careful consideration.

Referral and advice

The Commissioner's office would inevitably receive requests for advice, advocacy and information from individual children and young people and from adults acting on their behalf, although given the services already available it would not seek them. There are already a number of national sources of help, advice and counselling for children and young people, and many local agencies.

ChildLine receives thousands of calls each year from children as young as under five up to 18, with the majority of callers being between 12 and 15. Most calls are about physical and/or sexual abuse, family relationships and bullying. In addition to listening to and counselling children on the telephone, ChildLine tries as far as possible, if agreement with the child is reached, to refer cases to a suitable place where emergency or long-term help can be given. Another aim of ChildLine is to ensure that children's voices are heard in the public domain. ChildLine has strongly supported the proposal for a statutory Children's Rights Commissioner:

> We would see a Children's Commissioner providing an invaluable role in taking forward issues for children. The relationship between ChildLine and the Commissioner could be formalised, as it is in other countries, and ChildLine would be keen to cooperate in developing our general concerns, as evidenced from our telephone calls, as well as supplying the Commissioner with our reports. It is interesting to note that in Norway, the Commissioner has a telephone hotline for children about issues and their views.

Given the overall aim of developing close contact with children, the Commissioner's office would need to respond to enquiries sensitively and effectively, although it will generally be most appropriate to refer requests to national or local organisations providing assistance to children or to particular complaints procedures.

The Commissioner's office should avoid where possible merely giving a child or young person who contacts the office another phone number to ring. With the permission of the child or young person the Commissioner's staff should pass the complaint or request directly on to the relevant body, where appropriate asking to be informed in due course of the outcome. Ideally, over time, the Commissioner's Office might become a 'one-stop shop' where children and young people would know they could seek referral to appropriate local advice and advocacy services.

The Commissioner would operate according to strict rules of confidentiality on any approaches from children and young people. Advice should not be given to an adult where this could conflict with the rights or interests of the child concerned.

The courts

The Commissioner would be able to assist with legal actions in exceptional cases, having powers to support and assist children, or where necessary adults or organisations acting on their behalf, in getting legal advice and taking legal action. In particular, the Commissioner should be able to assist children in taking proceedings under the Human Rights Act or making applications to the European Human Rights Court in Strasbourg, or any other proceedings related to the promotion of children's human rights.

The Commissioner's staff would need to include legally qualified people. If the Commissioner required specialist legal advice which was not available within the staff, it could be sought from outside sources, e.g. counsel.

The Commissioner should also have the power to initiate or participate in legal proceedings in his or her own name whenever he or she believes it is the best way to promote the interests of children and young people. This could obviate the need for litigation to be conducted by specific individuals, which may be particularly difficult or unwelcome for children and young people. It would be analogous to the power local authorities have to institute or participate in legal proceedings where they 'consider it expedient for the promotion or protection of the interests of the inhabitants of their area'.[18] Similarly the CRE, the EOC, the Disability Rights Commission and the Northern Ireland Human Rights Commission can institute legal proceedings in their own name in certain circumstances including persistent discrimination and discriminatory advertising.

The legislation establishing the Northern Ireland Human Rights Commission (see page 26) places certain limitations on the provision of assistance. The Commission may grant an application for assistance – legal advice, representation or other assistance – on any of the following grounds:

- that the case raises a question of principle
- that it would be unreasonable to expect the person to deal with the case without assistance because of its complexity, or because of the person's position in relation to another person involved, or for some other reason
- that there are other special circumstances which make it appropriate for the Commission to provide assistance.

In the case of children and particularly young children there are special difficulties in taking legal action, which justify an important role for the Commissioner.

Other activities

International cooperation

We would expect the Commissioner to exchange information and cooperate with the many bodies promoting the human rights of children in other countries and to coordinate with them on international lobbying for children's rights, especially within the European Union and Council of Europe. The Commissioner would become a member of the European Network of Ombudsmen for Children, which already includes independent human rights institutions for children in 14 countries (see Chapter 5, page 77).

Official inquiries

The Commissioner may wish to give evidence to official national and local inquiries affecting children and young people (eg child abuse inquiries, planning inquiries).

Grants to self-advocacy groups

The Commissioner should have a specific power to give grants to self-advocacy organisations of children and young people working to promote children's human rights or to events intended to promote self-advocacy. There seems no need for the Commissioner to have other grant-giving powers or to alter the way in which voluntary organisations working with and for children generally receive government grants.

Reporting under the UN Convention

The Commissioner should have a specific duty to consider and comment (before submission) on the report which the Government must make every five years to the Committee on the Rights of the Child on implementation of the Convention. The Government would be required to have regard to the Commissioner's comments. (The Commissioner may also at other times wish to draw the attention of the Committee to situations or events in the UK or to children's rights issues generally.)

The Committee has indicated that it welcomes comments from independent institutions. At the session before its examination of a state's report, a pre-sessional working group of Committee members meets privately to consider submissions from UN agencies and NGOs on the state's progress towards implementing the Convention. In several cases children's ombudspeople or commissioners have submitted written reports and met with the pre-sessional working group.

It is the state which is required to report under the Convention. The Commissioner, as an expert on the implementation of children's human rights, has an obvious contribution to make to the reporting process. But the Commissioner's essential independence emphasises that as well as commenting on the Government's report he or she should submit separate information to the Committee. In addition, the Commissioner would have a particular role in ensuring that the Committee's 'Concluding Observations' on successive reports are properly considered and followed up by Government and Parliament.

There are other Treaty Bodies, like the Committee on the Rights of the Child, which receive reports and monitor the implementation of other human rights treaties which the UK has ratified: the Human Rights Committee (International Covenant on Civil and Political Rights); the Committee on Economic, Social and Cultural Rights (International Covenant on Economic, Social and Cultural Rights); the Committee Against Torture (Convention Against Torture and Other Cruel, Inhuman or Degrading Treatment or Punishment); the Committee on the Elimination of Discrimination Against Women (Convention on the Elimination of All Forms of Discrimination against Women) and the Committee on the Elimination of Racial Discrimination (International Convention on the Elimination of All Forms of Racial Discrimination). The Commissioner would need to consider from the perspective of children whether UK reports under these Conventions were adequate, encouraging the Government to consult it on draft reports and considering making independent submissions to the Treaty Bodies when necessary.

The Commissioner should also keep under review any UK reporting under European Conventions for their relevance to children – for example the European Social Charter.

Structure and ways of working

Location

The Children's Rights Commissioner for England and his or her staff would have an office in London. Despite the extra costs involved it would have to be situated in London to promote the most effective links with government departments, Parliament, the headquarters of most children's and professional organisations, and other bodies. Links should be established with similar offices in Northern Ireland, Scotland and Wales. There is of course the possibility that UK-wide legislation could set out the basic powers and duties of Commissioners for the four countries, with the role of the individual commissioners adapted as appropriate in each country.

Reporting arrangements

To Government

The Commissioner would report to the relevant Cabinet minister on issues which come under that minister. This is essential to tie the Commissioner into decision-making structures. However, many of the Commissioner's reports would cover responsibilities crossing departmental boundaries. In addition to going to the various departments concerned, these should probably also go to the secretary of state for the department which has lead responsibility for children's issues – currently the Department of Health (which is also currently responsible for reporting under the Convention on the Rights of the Child). An alternative would be for the Commissioner to report through the Home Office, which is responsible for the Human Rights Act and also for coordinating UK reporting under other international instruments. On occasions the Commissioner may wish to report direct to the Prime Minister. If a Minister for Children were to be appointed and a

Children's Unit established within the Cabinet Office (as proposed in *Effective Government Structures for Children*) this would provide an obvious route for reporting on many issues.

To Parliament

The Commissioner's annual report would be presented to Parliament. As well as reporting on his or her own activities, the Commissioner could include in his or her annual report a general description of the current situation of children and young people in the UK and important developments affecting them in the past year, unless the Government could be persuaded to produce such a report, in which case the Commissioner's role would be to contribute to and comment on it.

As noted in Chapter 1, a Parliamentary Human Rights Committee is to be established. The Commissioner would need to give evidence to it and to select committees on children's rights issues and propose areas of concern for these committees to scrutinise.

Taking Children Seriously proposed that a Parliamentary Select Committee should be set up specifically relating to the Commissioner's activities. Given the existence of the new Human Rights Committee this now seems unlikely. The Commissioner should form a close relationship with the Committee which, through its ability to question ministers and civil servants, could monitor ministerial and departmental implementation of the Commissioner's recommendations. It would also help raise the Parliamentary profile of the Commissioner's work. The relationships between the Parliamentary Commissioner for Administration and the linked Select Committee, and that between the National Audit Office and the Public Accounts Committee, seem to be successful examples of a connection between independent statutory offices and select committees. (The creation of select committees is a matter for Parliament rather than the Government.)

We would expect the Commissioner to have a close informal relationship with the All Party Parliamentary Group for Children.

Public profile

The Commissioner would wish to maintain a high public profile and work closely with the media in highlighting issues affecting children and young people which should be of public concern. The Commissioner would aim to develop the positive potential of the media for monitoring, promoting and protecting the human rights of children: encouraging coverage of children's rights, participation of children in the media and reporting of their views, and challenging negative stereotyping and inappropriate identification of children.

Input from children and young people

As noted above (page 42) it is essential that there is direct contact with children and direct input from children and young people into all aspects of the Commissioner's work. The Commissioner will have to consult with children and young people on how best to achieve this, and consider various strategies. For example, he or she could organise local or national forums of children and young people to discuss his or her work. He or she could also ask advisory groups of children and young people to discuss priorities for the Commissioner's work and the stance the Commissioner should adopt on various issues; or a network of regional advisory groups could be set up to allow the involvement of more children and young people. Specialist advisory groups could be formed, perhaps of children in care, adopted children or disabled children. Any advisory groups or forums could either deal with the Commissioner's overall activities or be related to particular topics which the Commissioner was currently working on or proposing to work on. The Commissioner would also have to consider how to keep in touch with the needs of categories of children who cannot be directly represented in these ways for reasons of, say, age or severe learning difficulties.

The Commissioner would also maintain close contact with organisations of children and young people – like Article 12 and A National Voice, youth councils and other local organisations, and ones which involve children and young people or have them as members. He or she could also request feedback through publications read by children and young people, television or radio programmes which they watch or listen to, or directly through the Commissioner's own materials aimed at children and young people. In other countries children's ombudspeople have used the Internet to communicate with and consult children. The Commissioner might also wish to conduct opinion research amongst children and young people on certain topics.

Input from children and young people into the Commissioner's work would of course also come from their letters, phone calls and e-mails, from direct contact through other parts of the Commissioner's work such as investigations, and through information on the concerns and complaints which are received from children and young people by other bodies (see page 54).

Liaison with outside organisations

The Commissioner would maintain close links with voluntary bodies and professional associations as well as statutory agencies involved with children and young people. The Commissioner would clearly wish to keep in close touch with developments on the ground and to benefit from the knowledge and expertise of others. The Commissioner may wish to organise regular meetings, conferences or seminars with such groups, either on particular topics or to discuss his or her activities in general. He or she might wish to hold an annual discussion forum on his or her work. The Children's Rights Alliance for England, formed in 1999, would be a key forum to relate to and work with.

Staffing and funding

The Commissioner would appoint his or her own staff of people fully committed to the principles of the UN Convention. He or she will require staff with specialist knowledge of law, policy and practice affecting children and young people, and who can take responsibility for particular policy areas. The Commissioner will also need staff with the following functions among others: investigations, media and PR work, information, liaison with outside bodies, and finance and internal support and administration. The Commissioner would also be able to use and pay for specialist advice from outside consultants as necessary. He or she may want to take on outside specialists to assist with particular reports and investigations, given the range of issues and services covered.

The Commissioner's remit is wide, and careful prioritisation of work will be essential. The level of resources available to the Commissioner will be important, and the greater those resources the greater will be the number of issues within the many possible areas of concern that the Commissioner is able to tackle effectively.

The Commissioner's office could either be funded through a separate Vote (as applies to some public bodies) or through a departmental budget, which could be that of the Department of Health or the Home Office. The advantage of the former route seems to be that it generally offers greater stability and more independence, whereas in the latter case a powerful and sympathetic secretary of state may be able to win greater resources.

Method of appointment

The Commissioner would be formally appointed by the Queen on the recommendation of the Secretary of State for Health or the Home Secretary. To maximise the Commissioner's protection from political and particularly government pressure, he or she could only be removed following resolutions of both Houses of Parliament. Many other appointments to public offices where independence is required have a similar safeguard. The Commissioner would be appointed for a renewable fixed term, probably five years. In making the appointment the personal attributes of candidates such as commitment to the principles of the Convention on the Rights of the Child, a wide understanding of the circumstances of children and services provided for them, the ability to form and maintain effective relationships with ministers and other bodies, and the ability to communicate well with children and through the media, will be more important than specific qualifications. The post should be advertised and subject to open competition. Alternatively the appointment should be made after consultation with relevant organisations including voluntary bodies committed to promoting and protecting children's rights.

Creating the Commissioner

Legislation will be required to establish the Commissioner and to ensure the office is created on a stable, independent basis and with the necessary legal powers and duties. Chapter 4 provides a model Bill.

1 See, for example, Kathleen Marshall, *Children's Rights in the Balance: The Participation-Protection Debate* (Edinburgh, The Stationery Office, 1997), pp. 54–63.

2 Children Act 1989, section 1(2).

3 Article 12, Voluntary Action Centre, 7 Mansfield Road, Nottingham NG1 3FB (tel. 0115 9348466); A National Voice, PO Box 253, Leeds LS1 2RL.

4 Disability Rights Commission Act 1999, section 4.

5 For more detailed discussion see Rachel Hodgkin and Peter Newell, *Effective Government Structures for Children* (London, Calouste Gulbenkian Foundation, 1996), p. 48 *et seq.*

6 Rachel Hodgkin, *Child Impact Statements 1997–98: An experiment in child-proofing UK Parliamentary Bills*, All Party Parliamentary Group for Children, UNICEF (London, National Children's Bureau, 1999), p. 31.

7 See note 6, p. 31.

8 Ministry for the Flemish Community, decree instituting an impact-report with regard to children and the monitoring of government policy in terms of its respect for the rights of the child, 15 July 1997.

9 *Strategy for the implementation of the UN Convention on the Rights of the Child in Sweden*, Ministry of Health and Social Affairs, Factsheet 1, January 1999.

10 Ombudsman Amendment (Child Protection and Community Services) Act 1998, New South Wales, Australia; see website www.nswombudsman.nsw.gov.au

11 See note 5, p. 53 *et seq.* for further discussion.

12 Concluding Observations of the Committee on the Rights of the Child on the initial report of the UK, CRC/C/15/Add.34, January 1995, para.26.

13 General guidelines regarding the form and contents of periodic reports to be submitted by States Parties under article 44, paragraph 1(b), of the Convention, Committee on the Rights of the Child, CRC/C/58, adopted 11 October 1996, para. 22.

14 Richard Bourne *et al.*, *School based understanding of human rights in four countries* (London, Department for International Development, 1998). Reported in Sarah Spencer and Ian Bynoe, *A Human Rights Commission: The options for Britain and Northern Ireland* (London, Institute for Public Policy Research, 1998).

15 *The Final Report of the Citizenship Advisory Group*, chaired by Sir Bernard Crick (Department for Education and Employment, London, 1998).

16 *One scandal too many..., the case for comprehensive protection of children in all settings*, Report of a Working Party convened by the Gulbenkian Foundation (London, Calouste Gulbenkian Foundation, 1993).

17 Under section 23 of the Education Reform Act 1988 – now consolidated in the Education Act 1996, section 409.

18 See Local Government Act 1972, section 222.

Chapter 3

A separate or integrated Children's Rights Commissioner?

The mission, guiding principles and activities set out in the previous chapter could be pursued either by a separate office of Children's Rights Commissioner or by a Commissioner integrated into a Human Rights Commission.

Within Europe, the following states have independent offices set up through legislation specifically to promote the human rights of children: Austria, Belgium (Flemish community), Denmark, Iceland, Norway, Russian Federation, Sweden and, in Spain, Madrid and Catalonia. Other states, including France, Germany, Ireland, Latvia, Poland and Switzerland are considering (in 1999) establishing such offices. In some other European countries – Hungary, Portugal, Spain and the Ukraine – specialist offices for children have been established within national human rights bodies (see Chapter 5, page 75).

The obvious advantages of a separate office are that it has a single-minded focus on the human rights of children, maximising the visibility of children and their rights and compensating for children's particular lack of political power. A possible disadvantage is that it could place children outside mainstream human rights advocacy and lose opportunities for joint working, for example on issues of race, disability and gender.

If it is decided to establish a Human Rights Commission for England or for the UK with separate Commissions in England, Northern Ireland, Scotland and Wales, and to integrate promotion and protection of children's rights into them, then it is essential that:

- the design and development of the Commission takes full account of the special status of children
- the legislation establishing the Commission is linked explicitly to implementation of the Convention on the Rights of the Child (thus covering children's economic, social and cultural rights as well as civil and political rights)
- the legislation includes provisions setting out specific functions, powers and duties relating to children, linked to the Convention. For example:
  - the duty to pay particular regard to the views and feelings of children and to take active steps to maintain direct contact with children
  - power to have regard to the situation of children in the family, in schools and other institutions
  - power to consider the promotion and protection of children's rights in relation not only to government but also private bodies

- the right to have access to children in all forms of alternative care and all institutions which include children
    - the right to report separately on the state of children's human rights
- there is an identifiable Children's Rights Commissioner for each country (ideally someone who will bring status and public and political respect to the office, have a high public profile and so enhance the status and visibility of children; and also be popular with children themselves)
- this individual has appropriate staffing dedicated to the promotion and protection of children's human rights and a ring-fenced minimum budget, and is able to attract and use funding from sources other than government.

Chapter 4 sets out a draft Bill to establish a Children's Rights Commissioner for England. If the post were to be integrated into a Human Rights Commission, some of the necessary powers and duties would be covered in general legislation (as is already the case in the law establishing the Northern Ireland Human Rights Commission), but there would be a need for some specific provisions too.

A SEPARATE OR INTEGRATED CHILDREN'S RIGHTS COMMISSIONER?

There is no overwhelming case for separation or for integration. The debate should revolve around establishing an office that can pursue the promotion and protection of children's human rights effectively, and ensuring that a Commissioner, whether integrated or separate, has the necessary profile, powers and duties. Below we set out some of the advantages and disadvantages of the two approaches as a basis for discussion:

A SEPARATE OFFICE

Advantages
- Able to take a distinctive and exclusive children's perspective.
- Provides a high-profile individual(s) to whom children can relate.
- Designed specifically to relate to children – in touch with children's views and feelings.
- Emphasises the priority which should be accorded to children.
- Able to take on specific tasks relevant to the particular situation of children (for example, certain child protection functions).
- Guarantees a distinct budget devoted to children's rights.

Disadvantages
- Lack of integration with mainstream human rights promotion.
- Possibility of marginalisation/lower status/fewer powers than national human rights institutions.
- Possible lack of adequate resources.
- Presents obstacle to effective joint working on inquiries, training, one-stop-shop advice services and promotion of human rights as a universal concept.

INTEGRATION

Advantages
- Able to integrate the promotion of children's rights into the mainstream promotion of all human rights.
- Can ensure that discussion of children's rights is not marginalised or accorded lesser status.
- Even where resources may not be adequate to support a range of separate offices, a Children's Commissioner within a Human Rights Commission would be able to use the power and resources of the whole institution.
- Able to work closely with other commissioners, for example on race or disability issues.
- A named Children's Rights Commissioner could ensure a specific individual with a personal profile for children to relate to.

Disadvantages
- Children's concerns tend to get lost in adult agendas.
- Children may not identify with and use an institution primarily designed for adults.
- Problems over implementation of children's rights often arise through conflicts between children and adults. A separate office would have more freedom to advocate from the child's perspective.
- National human rights institutions may be limited to reviewing only issues arising from an individual's relationship with the state; respect for children's rights also requires consideration of their relationship with those in authority over them: in the family, in schools and other institutions.

Which would be better for children? Current experience in some other European countries suggests that children's interests may be better served by a separate institution – but that is because insufficient attention has been given as yet to designing an effective integrated Commission with a specific focus on children. Internationally, the Office of the United Nations High Commissioner for Human Rights and UNICEF are promoting the development of a specific focus on the human rights of children within national human rights commissions, and there are positive models (see box below).

PROMOTING CHILDREN'S RIGHTS WITHIN NATIONAL HUMAN RIGHTS INSTITUTIONS – TWO EXAMPLES:

Philippines: Child Rights Centre in the Philippine Commission on Human Rights

The Philippine Commission on Human Rights was established through the 1987 Constitution. In 1994 the Child Rights Centre was established, initially with a grant from UNICEF. Its functions include:

- investigation of complaints of children's rights violations and initiation of legal action on behalf of children

- development and implementation of advocacy programmes on children's rights
- monitoring Government compliance with relevant international treaties
- mainstreaming promotion of children's rights within all the services of the Commission on Human Rights – investigation, jail visiting, legal assistance, education and public information programmes.

The Child Rights Centre focuses particularly on the civil rights and freedoms and special protection articles in the Convention on the Rights of the Child. In its first four years it has been preoccupied with issues concerning children in situations of armed conflict; it has also developed advocacy programmes for children in conflict with the law. Regional offices of the Commission on Human Rights have child rights desks and investigators. Within the education and training programme of the Commission, 15 per cent of the training modules for the police and military concern children's rights.

The Child Rights Centre has experienced difficulties in establishing a ring-fenced budget and sufficient resources to fulfil its mandate.

Australia: work of the Human Rights and Equal Opportunity Commission on children's rights

The Commission was established in its current form in 1986 as a federal body responsible for the protection of human rights in Australia. Commissioners have responsibility for particular portfolio areas such as sex discrimination, race discrimination and Indigenous social justice. The Human Rights Commissioner has the broadest responsibilities, covering those areas outside the specific portfolios of the other commissioners, and including children's rights (the other Commissioners will promote the rights of children within their specific mandates).

The Human Rights Commissioner has three full-time staff in his policy unit, one having a particular focus on children's rights. The children's rights budget, excluding salaries of the staff and Commissioner, is less than A$100,000 per annum.

Since 1993 the Convention on the Rights of the Child has been one of the international instruments to which the Commission is required to have regard. Functions in relation to children's rights include:

- investigating complaints about the practices of the Commonwealth that may be inconsistent with children's rights
- investigating complaints of discrimination in employment and occupation on the ground of age
- preparing guidelines for the avoidance of acts and practices that may be inconsistent with children's rights
- examining existing or proposed laws to ascertain their consistency or otherwise with children's rights
- intervening in court proceedings that involve children's rights
- undertaking research in areas relevant to children's rights
- public education and other activities to promote an understanding and acceptance of children's rights

- monitoring Australia's compliance with the Convention on the Rights of the Child.

The Commission has contributed detailed submissions to government and parliamentary inquiries – for example on the Convention and on child care funding – and advice on legislative proposals. It has undertaken inquiries into patterns of human rights violations, including inquiries into children and the legal process, rural and remote school education, and homeless children. Participation of children has become a central theme of the Commission's work. It has established reference groups to advise it on particular projects, undertaken surveys of children, held focus groups at schools and youth groups and developed educational and promotional material in a form that children can easily relate to. This includes specialised children's versions of Commission reports and publications.

As indicated above (and in Chapter 5, page 75) some European countries have established separate children's rights commissioners or ombudsmen for children and some have developed arrangements for promotion of children's rights within a national human rights institution. It is undoubtedly possible to develop a distinctive and effective children's rights commissioner within a broader human rights institution. The debate needs to move beyond 'separation or integration' to a detailed consideration of the necessary powers, duties and design of the commissioner and of the commission and its management structures to ensure the right balance between distinct functions for children and joint working.

At the time of writing (September 1999), the Northern Ireland Human Rights Commission was in the process of drafting a Strategic Plan, and determining what sort of priority to give to children's rights within its limited resources. Thus Northern Ireland's 500,000 children and young people are the first in the UK to have a statutory human rights institution (see Chapter 1, page 26 for more details). Advocacy for the establishment of a free-standing children's rights commissioner with similar statutory powers to the Commission and particular obligations to promote and protect the human rights of children continues in Northern Ireland, alongside advocacy to create a distinct focus for children within the Human Rights Commission.

The legislation in the Northern Ireland Act makes no specific mention of children; the term 'human rights' as defined in the Act includes, but is not limited to, the rights in the European Human Rights Convention, now incorporated into UK domestic law through the Human Rights Act 1998. The mission statement of the NI Commission refers broadly to 'internationally accepted rules and principles for the protection of human rights'. While the general powers would enable the NI Commission to fulfil some of the specific functions relating to the promotion and protection of children's human rights set out above (page 64), the legislation does not include any of the proposed specific provisions; there is no requirement to appoint a children's rights commissioner.

If it is decided to develop promotion of children's rights in Northern Ireland within the Human Rights Commission, the current legislation could be amended appropriately.

Chapter 4

A Bill to create a Children's Rights Commissioner

In July 1999 Hilton Dawson MP and others representing all major parties were given leave in the House of Commons to introduce under the 'Ten-minute Rule' a Bill 'to provide for the establishment of a children's rights commissioner to promote the rights and interests of children in England; to make provision for the powers and duties of the commissioner and for related purposes.'

The Bill had no hope of making progress, but its presentation marks a new step towards establishing an effective body to promote and protect the human rights of children.

The following is the text of the Bill, which provides a framework of duties and powers reflecting the mission, principles and activities outlined in Chapter 2.

ARRANGEMENT OF CLAUSES

Clause
1. Appointment and staff of Commissioner.
2. Duties and guiding principles.
3. Annual reports.
4. Recommendations and compliance notices.
5. Following up recommendations.
6. Investigations.
7. Child impact statements.
8. Complaints procedures.
9. Other powers and functions.
10. Legal proceedings and inquiries.
11. Legislation affecting children.
12. Code of consultation.
13. Minister's requests.
14. Reports to Committee on the Rights of the Child.
15. Review of Act.
16. Interpretation.
17. Financial provisions.
18. Short title and extent.

A

B I L L

TO

Provide for the establishment of a children's rights commissioner to promote the rights and interests of children in England; to make provision for the powers and duties of the commissioner; and for related purposes.

A.D. 1999.

BE IT ENACTED by the Queen's most Excellent Majesty, by and with the advice and consent of the Lords Spiritual and Temporal, and Commons, in this present Parliament assembled, and by the authority of the same, as follows:—

5   **1.**—(1) There shall be a Children's Rights Commissioner, who shall be appointed by Her Majesty on the recommendation of the Secretary of State.

   (2) Before making such a recommendation the Secretary of State shall consult such persons as appear to him to be appropriate.

   (3) The Commissioner—

10   (a) shall be appointed for a period of five years;

     (b) shall hold office during that period unless—

        (i) relieved at his own request; or

        (ii) removed by Her Majesty in consequence of addresses from both Houses of Parliament;

15   (c) at the end of a term of appointment shall be eligible for reappointment.

   (4) The Commissioner may appoint such staff as he thinks fit to assist with the discharge of his functions; and any function of the Commissioner may be performed by any member of his staff authorised for that purpose by 20 the Commissioner.

   (5) The Commissioner and the Commissioner's staff shall not be regarded as agents or servants of the Crown.

   2.—(1) The Commissioner shall be under a duty—

     (a) to promote the rights and interests of children;

Appointment and staff of Commissioner.

Duties and guiding principles.

(b) to seek to ensure that the rights and interests of children are properly taken into account by Ministers of the Crown, government departments, local authorities, other public bodies and voluntary and private organisations when decisions on policies affecting children are taken; 5

(c) to promote compliance with the United Nations Convention on the Rights of the Child as ratified by Her Majesty's Government and subject to such reservations as Her Majesty's Government made on ratification, unless subsequently withdrawn; and

(d) to seek to ensure that children have effective means of redress if 10 their rights are disregarded by any body referred to in paragraph (b).

(2) In exercising these functions the Commissioner shall have regard to—

(a) the principles laid down in the United Nations Convention on the Rights of the Child, and in such other international treaties, 15 conventions or agreements which have been ratified or otherwise acceded to by Her Majesty's Government and which affect children;

(b) the need to maintain direct contact with children and children's organisations, to pay particular regard to the views of children and 20 to promote respect for the views of children throughout society;

(c) the need to ensure co-ordination between different bodies (including government departments) which provide services for children; and

(d) the need to consult from time to time other persons seeking to promote the rights and interests of children. 25

Annual reports.

3.—(1) As soon as practicable after the end of each calendar year the Commissioner shall submit an annual report on his activities during the year to the Secretary of State.

(2) An annual report shall include a general description of the circumstances of children in England and a survey of developments which 30 have affected them during the period of the report.

(3) The Secretary of State shall lay a copy of each annual report before both Houses of Parliament and shall cause the report to be published.

Recommendations and compliance notices.

4.—(1) The Commissioner may make other reports at his discretion, and may publish them as he thinks fit; and such reports may contain such 35 recommendations for action by others (including Ministers of the Crown) as in the opinion of the Commissioner are necessary or expedient.

(2) In making recommendations under subsection (1) the Commissioner shall give reasons in the report and shall send a copy of the report to any person at whom a recommendation is directed. 40

(3) If it appears to the Commissioner that a person is not complying with the provisions of the United Nations Convention on the Rights of the Child as ratified by Her Majesty's Government he may make recommendations in the form of a compliance notice, which shall state his opinion as to the way in which provisions in the Convention are not being complied with and what 45 action should be taken to comply.

5.—(1) A person at whom a recommendation is directed by a Commissioner shall—

Following up recommendations.

    (a) consider the recommendation; and

    (b) notify the Commissioner within three months of receiving it (or a longer period if the Commissioner agrees) of the action which has been taken or it is intended to take in response to the recommendation.

(2) Where a person at whom a recommendation is directed intends not to comply with it he shall furnish the Commissioner with reasons for not doing so; and the Commissioner may publish the reasons.

(3) The Commissioner may require a person at whom a recommendation is directed to furnish him with such information as may be reasonably required to verify whether the recommendation has been complied with.

(4) Any person who fails to comply (whether wholly or partly) with a compliance notice may be required to publish that failure in such manner as the Commissioner may specify.

(5) If the Commissioner has reasonable cause for believing that a person will not comply with subsection (4) he may—

    (a) publish the failure to comply with the notice; and

    (b) recover from that person any reasonable expenses incurred.

(6) The Commissioner shall—

    (a) establish and maintain a register of compliance notices; and

    (b) ensure that the register may be inspected at all reasonable hours by any person.

6.—(1) The Commissioner may conduct a formal investigation for any purpose connected with the carrying out of his duties.

Investigations.

(2) For the purposes of a formal investigation the Commissioner may require any person who possesses documents or information relevant to the investigation to—

    (a) produce such documents;

    (b) furnish the information in writing;

    (c) attend at a specified time and place and give oral information.

(3) No person shall be compelled under subsection (2) to give information or produce documents which he could not be compelled to give or produce in civil proceedings before the High Court.

(4) The Commissioner shall prepare and publish a report of his findings in any formal investigation and shall include in it such recommendations as appear to him to be necessary or expedient.

7.—(1) Whenever it appears necessary or expedient to the Commissioner, he may require a Minister of the Crown to provide a child impact statement relating to any decision or proposal on policy which the Minister has made and which affects or may affect children.

Child impact statements.

(2) A child impact statement under subsection (1) shall set out the probable impact in the Minister's opinion on children of the decision or

proposal to which the statement relates; and the Minister shall cause the statement to be published.

(3) Where the Commissioner publishes his opinions with regard to a child impact statement and requests the Minister who provided the statement to respond to these opinions, the Minister shall comply with that request.   5

Complaints procedures.

8.—(1) The Commissioner may require any person who is under a statutory duty to establish, operate or supervise any procedure for the consideration of representations or complaints to provide such information as can reasonably be obtained about the number, nature and outcomes of representations or complaints made by or on behalf of children.   10

(2) The Commissioner may request such information from any person who has established, operates or supervises any other procedure for the consideration of representations or complaints.

(3) Information provided to the Commissioner under subsection (1) or (2) shall not identify any person who has made a representation or complaint.   15

Other powers and functions.

9.—(1) Where the Commissioner considers it necessary or expedient for the carrying out of his duties, he may—

(a) publish and disseminate information about children;

(b) undertake or assist (financially or otherwise) the undertaking by other persons of any research;   20

(c) give assistance to a child or to a person acting on behalf of a child, which may include giving advice (including legal advice) or arranging for legal advice or for legal representation;

(d) give financial or other assistance to any organisation for the purpose of encouraging the promotion by children of the interests of   25
children.

(2) In deciding whether to give assistance under subsection (1)(c) the Commissioner shall have regard to—

(a) the availability of such assistance elsewhere;

(b) whether in the Commissioner's opinion an important question of   30
principle is involved; and

(c) what is in the Commissioner's opinion the most efficient and effective means for the discharge of his duties.

Legal proceedings and inquiries.

10. Where the Commissioner considers it necessary or expedient for the promotion or protection of the interests or rights of children, he may—   35

(a) prosecute or defend or appear in any legal proceedings and, in the case of civil proceedings, institute them in his own name;

(b) in his own name make representations in the interests of children at any public inquiry held by or on behalf of a Minister or public body under any enactment.   40

Legislation affecting children.

11.—(1) If a Minister of the Crown proposes—

(a) to present a Bill which seeks to amend or repeal the whole or part of an enactment which significantly affects children; or

(b) to make a statutory instrument under any provision of an enactment where that provision significantly affects children

he shall first consult the Commissioner.

(2) The Secretary of State may by order specify which enactments and which provisions of which enactments are to be taken as significantly affecting children for the purposes of subsection (1).

(3) When the Commissioner is consulted under subsection (1) he shall—

(a) consider the Minister's proposals; and

(b) publish his response

and the Minister shall have regard to that response.

12.—(1) The Secretary of State shall with the agreement of the Commissioner produce a code of consultation setting out the circumstances in which government departments shall consult the Commissioner, together with guidance on the timing and method of such consultations, arrangements for publication, and any other relevant matters.

Code of consultation.

(2) Government departments shall have regard to a code of consultation under this section.

13. Where a Minister of the Crown requests the Commissioner to consider or report on a particular matter the Commissioner shall have regard to that request.

Minister's requests.

14. A draft of any report which Her Majesty's Government intends to submit to the Committee on the Rights of the Child under Article 44 of the United Nations Convention on the Rights of the Child shall be sent to the Commissioner, who shall consider it and respond; and Her Majesty's Government shall have regard to the Commissioner's response before submitting the report.

Reports to Committee on the Rights of the Child.

15. The Commissioner shall from time to time, when he thinks fit or is so required by the Secretary of State—

Review of Act.

(a) review the working of this Act; and

(b) submit to the Secretary of State any proposals for amending it.

16. In this Act "child" means a person under the age of eighteen.

Interpretation.

17. *There shall be paid out of money provided by Parliament any expenditure incurred—*

Financial provisions.

(a) by a Minister of the Crown;

(b) by the Children's Rights Commissioner

by virtue of this Act.

18.—(1) This Act may be cited as the Children's Rights Commissioner Act 1999.

Short title and extent.

(2) This Act extends only to England.

Chapter 5

Children's Rights Commissioners and similar offices in Europe

Across Europe, independent offices to promote and protect the human rights of children have been established in many countries. The development has accelerated in the context of implementation of the Convention on the Rights of the Child – ratified by all European countries – and encouragement from the Council of Europe. There is a European Network of Ombudsmen for Children – ENOC (see box, page 77) which aims to promote the development of effective new offices.

There is no single model or accepted definition of a children's ombudsman or children's rights commissioner. Existing offices vary in title, size, functions, in legislative powers and duties and in the degree of independence from government; some are federal, some regional and some local; some are free-standing and others form an integral part of a national human rights institution – a human rights commission or general ombudsman's office. In some countries different models operate at the federal and the regional level.

The first office to be established through legislation, the Norwegian Children's Ombudsman, was evaluated in 1995 and its Act was recently amended to link it to the Convention on the Rights of the Child. Sweden was the first state to establish a Children's Ombudsman with legislation directly linking it to implementation of the Convention, in 1993. The Office was evaluated in 1998–9 and the resulting report recommends more direct contact with children and young people and more independence. The Flemish community of Belgium is the first to use the title Children's Rights Commissioner for its independent office, established in 1998.

As with any evolving concept it is hard to draw lines and define what does and does not come within the definition of an independent institution to promote and protect the human rights of children.

For the purpose of deciding which offices should become members of ENOC, the Network agreed in 1999 to the following statement:

> ENOC recognises that the concept of independent offices for children - children's ombudsmen, commissioners and so on – is a developing one, and that its criteria for membership will need to be kept under review.
>
> Membership of ENOC is open to offices within Council of Europe member-countries which meet one of the following criteria:
>
> 1 Independent national or regional offices set up through legislation specifically to promote children's rights and interests.
> 2 Independent national or regional human rights institutions set up through legislation which include a specific focus on children's rights.

Thus the key characteristics for ENOC are independence and establishment through legislation. For 'general' national human rights institutions to qualify they must have an explicit focus on children's rights.

The 'Paris Principles' adopted by the UN General Assembly to guide the development of national human rights institutions place a particular emphasis on independence and on establishment through legislation (see Appendix 2, page 94, for text, and Chapter 1, page 16, for discussion). The Committee on the Rights of the Child has also stressed independence, and in some cases urged governments to give established offices greater independence (for example in relation to New Zealand's Commissioner for Children and Sweden's Children's Ombudsman – see page 20).

As noted in the general discussion of national human rights institutions in Chapter 1, non-governmental organisations (NGOs) play a key role in the independent promotion and protection of children's human rights. In Europe, the first office to use the title 'Children's Ombudsman' was established in the 1970s as part of Radda Barnen, Swedish Save the Children. In Finland, a very large children's NGO, the Mannerheim League for Child Welfare, operates a Children's Ombudsman Office, as does Israel's National Council for the Child, also an NGO. And in 1999 an Office of Children's Rights Commissioner for London was established as a three-year demonstration project to make the case for a statutory Commissioner (see page 34). None of these offices has legislative powers and so they do not meet the requirements of the Paris Principles, nor ENOC's membership criteria. The concept of an independent statutory office for children, promoted in this book, is complementary to the role of NGOs; an office given specific legislative powers and duties.

In many countries there are also now Parliamentary bodies promoting children's rights. Germany's KinderKommission, for example, brings representatives of Germany's major political parties together to work on children's issues. Other states have Parliamentary Committees on children and special hearings in Parliament on children's issues and involving children. In the UK there is the All Party Parliamentary Group on Children.

It is plain that worldwide some offices – for example New Zealand's Commissioner for Children, the Children's Interests Bureau in South Australia and children's ombudspeople in New South Wales and Queensland – have been initiated more from a child welfare and child protection perspective than a children's rights perspective. In some countries, too, offices are in effect agencies of the government, although they may be permitted to operate with some degree of independence.

The following section provides details of a selection of the offices in Europe, and a summary of progress towards establishing offices. (Examples of legislation establishing some of the offices are given in Appendix 3, page 98).

EUROPEAN NETWORK OF OMBUDSMEN FOR CHILDREN

The European Network of Ombudsmen for Children, ENOC, was formed in Trondheim, Norway in 1997, initially with independent offices for children in 10 countries. UNICEF's Office for Europe in Geneva acts as the Secretariat. ENOC – 'a new voice for children in Europe' – aims 'to improve the lives of all children in Europe' in ways which include:

- encouraging the fullest possible implementation of the UN Convention on the Rights of the Child
- supporting individual and collective lobbying for children's rights and interests to Europe-wide and international bodies
- sharing information, approaches and strategies for the benefit of children, including comparative studies
- providing a forum for individual offices to generate new ideas and gain support
- promoting and supporting the development of effective offices able to advocate independently for children
- acting collectively to ensure positive national policies for children
- monitoring the state of children and the impact of political and economic changes on children.

A website, providing details of ENOC's member-offices, their activities and position statements developed by the Network, is at www.ombudsnet.org

A SUMMARY OF EXISTING OFFICES IN EUROPE

Austria: the Youth Welfare Act 1989 promoted the establishment of local ombudspeople in each of the nine *Länder* (regions) for children under the age of 18. Each *Land* has developed its own legislation. The nine children's ombudsmen form a 'Conference of Ombudsmen' to respond on federal issues; additionally a federal children's ombudsperson (*Kinder- und Jugendanwalt des Bundes*) was introduced in 1991 – an official in the Ministry of Environment, Youth and the Family.

Belgium: the Council of the French Community established a *Délégué Général aux Droits de L'enfant* (General Delegate for Children's Rights) in 1991. The General Delegate is appointed by the Executive of the French Community. In the Flemish Community a decree was passed by the Flemish Parliament in 1997 establishing a Children's Rights Commissioner and a Commission (the Commissioner and staff).

Denmark: a National Council for Children was set up in 1994 for a three-year trial period as an independent body based on the Ministry of Social Affairs. After evaluation it became a permanent body by an Order issued by the Minister. Three members including the Chair are appointed by the Minister; the remaining four by the coalition of children's NGOs.

Hungary: within the Office of the Parliamentary Commissioner for Human Rights, the Deputy Commissioner covers children's issues and there is a small specialist staff.

Iceland: an Ombudsman for Children was established by statute in 1995, linked to implementation of the Convention.

Norway: the world's first legislation establishing an office of Children's Ombudsman (Barneombudet) was passed by the Norwegian Parliament in 1981.

Portugal: the Portuguese Ombudsman for Justice (Provedoria de Justiça) has specific staff covering children's issues and responding to children's inquiries and complaints (there is a telephone 'hotline' for children).

Russian Federation: Five of the 89 regions of the Russian Federation – city regions or 'oblasts' – have appointed children's ombudsmen or commissioners for children's rights: City of Ekaterinburg (population 1 million; child population 200,000); Kaluga Oblast (population 1 million; child population 220,000); Novgorod Oblast (population 740,000; child population 150,000); St Petersburg (population 4.7 million; child population 850,000); Volgograd Oblast (population 2.7 million; 600,000 children).

These offices have been initiated through a joint project of the Federal Ministry of Labour and Social Development and UNICEF.

Spain: the national human rights institution includes an office for children's rights; in addition an Ombudsman for Children has been established by legislation in Madrid (*Defensor del Menor en la Comunidad de Madrid*). In the autonomous region of Catalonia a General Ombudsman was created by law in 1984 and in 1989 the law was modified to allow for the post of Deputy for Children.

Sweden: established the Office of the Children's Ombudsman, with statutory powers linked to the UN Convention, in 1993.

The Ukraine: a Parliamentary Delegate for Human Rights was appointed in April 1998 and plans to appoint a Representative for Children's Rights through a Parliamentary decree.

In other European countries proposals for an independent office for children are under consideration by government, including in **France**, **Germany**, **Ireland**, **Latvia**, **Poland** and **Switzerland**.

A SUMMARY OF EXISTING OFFICES IN OTHER CONTINENTS

Australia: the federal Human Rights and Equal Opportunities Commission has a mandate which includes the Convention on the Rights of the Child and dedicated staff covering children's rights issues; in **New South Wales** in 1998 the general Ombudsman was given some specific functions relating to child protection; in particular to oversee and monitor the handling of child abuse investigations and convictions against employees of certain government and non-government agencies providing care and/or education for children: in **Queensland** a Children's Commissioner with particular child protection functions was established in 1997 by statute; in **South Australia** the Children's Interests Bureau opened in 1984, established under the Community Welfare Amendment Act. But in 1995 it suffered some curbs on its independence, when it was amalgamated with the Office for Families and the Domestic Violence Unit, to create the Office for Families and Children.

Canada: in **British Columbia** the Ombudsman Services created a new post of Deputy Ombudsman for Children and Youth in 1987, but the specific role for children ceased to exist in 1990 and was absorbed into the general remit. In **Alberta and some other provinces** Children's Advocates have been set up under child welfare legislation to advocate on behalf of children who are receiving child protection services.

Costa Rica: an ombudsman office for children was established under the jurisdiction of the Ministry of Justice in 1987; in 1993 the various specialised ombudsman offices were incorporated into a national independent ombudsman office (*Defensor de los Habitantes de la República*) which includes a children's unit.

Guatemala: the children's ombudsperson, *Defensor de los Derechos de la Niñez*, was set up as a special unit of a new government office established to investigate human rights under the constitution of 1986.

New Zealand: a statutory Commissioner for Children was created in 1989.

Philippines: a Child Rights Centre was established within the Human Rights Commission in 1995; it investigates violations of children's rights, initiates legal action on behalf of children, develops advocacy programmes, monitors compliance with international treaties and mainstreams the children's rights agenda in the various services of the Commission.

South Africa: the Deputy Chairperson of the South African Human Rights Commission (SAHRC) also acts as Chairperson of the SAHRC Standing Committee on Child Rights.

Norway

Norway was the first country to use legislation to establish a children's ombudsman, by Act of Parliament in 1981. Norway's population is just over four million. The King (in practice the Cabinet) appoints the Ombudsman for a term of four years, and he or she can be reappointed for a second term only. Norway has a Ministry of Children and Family Affairs, and it is through this Ministry that the office is financed. The office started with just two staff in 1981, but grew quite quickly. Now there are 10 permanent positions and a varying number of short-term project workers. The annual budget is about £540,000.

There was an evaluation of the office in 1993 which was generally very positive. It proposed a shift of focus even further from individual problems towards policy development on behalf of children as a group. The evaluation committee found that the Ombudsman had helped to put the political spotlight on children, both by putting children on, and by moving them up, the political agenda. The Ombudsman had particularly helped to improve laws affecting children in institutions, refugee children and school students. It had become a universally known and very popular office. The committee also noted that the idea of the Children's Ombudsman had been a good export. It proposed that it would be useful to link the Ombudsman's role to the Convention – because establishment of the Office pre-dated the Convention – and the 1981 Act was revised in 1998 to bring in the Convention. (The law and Standing Instructions for the Ombudsman are reproduced in Appendix 3, page 98).

Changes which the first Ombudsman helped to achieve in her term of office from 1981 to 1989 included:

- new regulations for hospitalised children, in the areas of contact with parents and of education
- raising the age at which children can be imprisoned in adult prisons
- legislation prohibiting all physical punishment of children
- a requirement that all local planning authorities have a special official responsible for monitoring plans for their impact on children
- legislative recognition of the right of children to know both their parents, regardless of parents' marital status
- tighter building regulations on safety for children in the home, and accident prevention.

In recent years the office has received over 20,000 individual approaches annually, the majority from children, by mail or by phone, using the free children's line. Recent activities of the office include setting up an 'Internet Parliament' with all the school democracy councils in primary and secondary schools. These electronic contacts enable the Ombudsman to consult children speedily on issues and policy proposals.

The Ombudsman is encouraging a big political debate on the future of schools, with a national hearing for secondary school students who were asked to come up with visions and ideas for the future of the education system.

With Save the Children in Norway, the Ombudsman has set up an international network to challenge the spread of child pornography through the Internet; an e-mail hotline to enable people to provide information.

Sweden

As long ago as 1809 the office of Parliamentary Ombudsman was established in Sweden, in connection with the introduction of the then new Constitution. Rather more recently various specialist ombudspeople have been appointed: Consumer Ombudsman, Equal Opportunities Ombudsman, Ombudsman against Ethnic Discrimination, Children's Ombudsman, Disability Ombudsman and the Ombudsman against Discrimination because of Sexual Orientation.

Radda Barnen, the Swedish Save the Children, a large NGO, ran an Ombudsman office for a few years from the 1970s as a demonstration project, and promoted the idea internationally. In 1993 the Government decided to establish a Children's Ombudsman by Act of Parliament. There is a very short two-section Act, and more detailed Standing Instructions expand on the Ombudsman's duties (see Appendix 3, page 102).

The office is not permitted to take on individual cases or complaints at all – it is there to provide children as a group with a voice (Sweden's population is almost nine million). The budget of the office is roughly the same as Norway's, and there is an Ombudsman with a staff of up to 18, including lawyers, statisticians, social workers and a press officer.

Sweden's office has had a particular focus on local implementation of the Convention: it carried out two surveys in 1995 and 1997 on the extent to which the Convention is known about and implemented locally. It publishes a handbook for local politicians and officials on how to implement the Convention and has also circulated all central government agencies, quangos and so on, promoting implementation. It has used an Internet site to seek children's views. In connection with Sweden's second report under the Convention on the Rights of the Child the Ombudsman prepared a report for the Committee on the Rights of the Child and attended the meeting of the Committee's pre-sessional working group to comment on implementation in Sweden.

The Ombudsman lobbied for a National Council on Child Abuse and Neglect and the Government agreed to appoint a parliamentary committee; the Ombudsman is a member. She has a national coordinating role on child safety and has recently looked at particular problems of accidents in daycare centres.

Following a detailed report by a Swedish Parliamentary Committee on the compatibility of the state's law, policy and practice with the Convention, the Swedish Parliament adopted a Bill in 1999 which is in effect a national strategy for implementing the Convention, giving the Ombudsman a major role in it.

Evaluation of the Ombudsman

In 1998 the Government appointed a one-man Committee of Inquiry to review the activities of the Ombudsman, with a secretariat, special advisers and experts from departments and government agencies attached to it and a reference group of young people aged 15 to 16. The intention was that the evaluation should describe how the office of the Children's Ombudsman might be strengthened and its activities made more effective. The conclusions of this recent and detailed evaluation are of particular interest to those seeking to develop an independent human rights institution for children now.

The Committee states that the Children's Ombudsman has:

- played a significant role in the development of issues relating to children, chiefly through information and opinion-moulding activities
- made visible the overall living conditions of children and young people and helped to create a comprehensive picture of their lives
- brought momentum to the task of implementing the CRC
- been most effective in upholding children's rights when she has been in a position to act as their representative and been able to refer to their experiences and views.

But the Committee also found weaknesses in the mandate and direction of work of the Ombudsman:

- no legal powers
- limited opportunity to build up networks and contacts in her capacity as the representative of children and young people – in particular, contacts with children and young people and people working with them.

The Committee suggests that the fundamental task of the Children's Ombudsman should be to represent children and young people:

> That is to say, to be the 'voice' of children and young people in society, to assert their point of view and insist on respect for their human rights. Children whose situation is precarious in one way or another find it particularly difficult to make themselves heard and influence their situation. Therefore it is the view of the Committee that the Children's Ombudsman should continue to devote special attention to issues relating to disadvantaged children.

The Ombudsman is representing the community's 'fundamental and common interest in ensuring that all children and young people are granted the rights set out in the UN Convention on the Rights of the Child'.

In order to apply a child perspective, the Ombudsman needs in-depth knowledge of the circumstances of children and the varying needs of different age groups:

> In the Committee's opinion, the Ombudsman should seek knowledge as close to children and young people as possible. This means that the most important source of knowledge must be children and young people themselves, parents, personnel who work with children and young people and organisations that run activities for children and young people.

The Committee believes that the task of developing direct contacts with children and young people is so vital that it should be confirmed in legislation. A prerequisite for developing contacts with children and young people is that the Ombudsman:

> should be allowed greater freedom of action and more opportunities to work flexibly. It is crucial that the Office of Children's Ombudsman has the opportunity to set its own agenda. Contacts with children and young people can never be based on the same structure as cooperation with public agencies and organisations. Such activities require great flexibility within the Ombudsman's own organisation.

The Committee emphasises that the Ombudsman must be independent in relation both to Government and to political parties: 'However, it is important to emphasise that a government-appointed ombudsman can never be completely independent. The law in combination with the power of the principal to make decisions about the Ombudsman's budget places certain constraints on the work of the Ombudsman.'

The report looks at the possibility of making the Ombudsman accountable to Parliament rather than, as at present, to Government. In either case it is essential that the office of Ombudsman achieves the highest degree of independence from its principal. The Committee comes down in favour of keeping the current accountability to Government, but increasing independence by setting out the duties and functions of the Ombudsman in law rather than instructions, and in particular by ensuring that the Ombudsman can decide his or her own agenda rather than being set tasks with attached budgets. It believes there are advantages in the close dialogue between the Ombudsman and the Minister most directly involved in implementation of children's rights.

> It is more difficult to envisage a dialogue with the Parliament in its role as principal, since all political parties with their various views are represented there. Since the practical implementation of the principles contained in the CRC is open to a variety

of political interpretations, the Children's Ombudsman could be forced to keep a lower profile if the Parliament were its principal than if it were accountable to a Government body.

The Committee further proposes that the Ombudsman should have the power to require information from agencies and local authorities and summon these bodies to talks; also a right of access to documents.

The Children's Ombudsman is the only ombudsman in Sweden who does not handle individual cases; the Committee proposes no change, on the grounds that handling individual cases 'would in all likelihood make such heavy demands on the time and resources of the Office that other activities would be pushed into the background'.

The Children's Ombudsman should 'spearhead' work on the Convention: 'Spearhead is used here to mean that the Ombudsman should be one step ahead of developments by having a cohesive body of knowledge about the living conditions of children and young people and by disseminating knowledge of best practices…' The main task should be to encourage children and young people to play an active role in the process of change: 'In order to ascertain the practical effect of work to implement the CRC it will be necessary to ask children and young people if they feel that their rights are being provided for.' The Ombudsman should increase efforts to ensure that 'children and young people know about the Ombudsman and perceive him or her to be their own Ombudsman'.

In its monitoring role, the Ombudsman should devote more time to considering how courts, public agencies and local authorities apply existing rules and regulations.

Iceland

Iceland's Children's Ombudsman was created by an Act in 1994, coming into effect in 1995 (Iceland's population is 263,000). The overall objective is to improve the position of children in society, and to defend their interests and rights; the office can investigate cases, but not disputes between individuals.

The Office prepares, annually, a 'State of Iceland's Children' report; it has focused in particular on child accidents, bullying and media violence. An analysis of all Iceland's laws which affect children has been written up in an accessible form for children – a children's book of laws.

Denmark

A rather different institutional model has developed in Denmark (population five million). In 1994 the National Council for Children was formed for a three-year trial period, coming from a proposal of NGOs and individuals. For 10 years there had been an unsuccessful campaign to establish a children's ombudsman; the Government did not accept the idea of specialist ombudsmen. So the NGOs proposed instead an independent Council to safeguard and promote children's interests. The Council has seven members. The Minister for Social Affairs appoints the chairman and two members; the other four are appointed by the NGOs concerned with children and their rights. In 1997, after the first three years, there was an evaluation, and the Council was then established in the law as a permanent institution.

The Council is there to advise on conditions affecting children; it must include children's points of view in its work. It is not permitted to take up individual complaints. The Danish Council has developed an elaborate form of consultation with children, establishing contacts with seven schools and a daycare institution (4–6 year olds) – 150 children in all. The children have agreed to consider and respond to questions and papers which the Council sends them. They discuss them with their teachers, and can then respond either individually or collectively. There have been consultations on children's employment and pay, children's use of videos and TV, children's participation in decision-making, both in the family and in local planning, and on corporal punishment in the family. The Council has also brought all the children together for residential conferences.

Current activities of the Council include a major 'no smacking' campaign following explicit prohibition of all corporal punishment of children in 1997. The Council together with Danish Save the Children lobbied extensively for this reform and all Danish parents with children in the age group 0–10 received a folder of materials on the law and on positive discipline. Work on anti-bullying has included promoting law reform, collection and circulation of good practice and mobilisation of children on the issue.

Austria

In Austria a new federal law in 1989 required the appointment of 'youth welfare agencies' to advise children, and to help in cases of conflict. The federal law left the regional administrations to decide what form these agencies should take. Each of the nine regions – *Länder* – had by 1995 established an office of Ombudsperson for Children and Youth (the populations of the regions vary from half a million to a million). There are differences in detail in the laws in different regions, but their functions are broadly similar and include generally representing the rights and interests of children, but also taking up individual cases and even representing children in court.

In 1993, the Austrian Conference of Ombudsmen was formed, and now the nine Ombudsmen and their staff meet at least three times a year, and are in frequent contact in between. One particular job for the Conference is to give an expert opinion on any proposed new federal laws that will affect children, and also to propose changes or new laws. There is also a federal Children's Ombudsman, an official in the Federal Ministry of Environment, Youth and the Family.

Belgium

In the French community, a General Delegate for the Rights of the Child was first appointed in 1991; the major work is responding to individual cases and complaints.

For the Flemish community, the Flemish Parliament passed a decree in 1997 establishing a Children's Rights Commissioner and Commission (the Commissioner and staff; see text of law in Appendix 3, page 105). The Commissioner had an initial staff of four. She is required to follow up implementation of the Convention; defend rights and interests of children in Flanders; analyse, evaluate and make public the conditions they live in. The Commissioner is required to establish a dialogue with children and with NGOs working for children's rights. She must examine complaints regarding non-compliance with the Convention and where possible refer to appropriate other institutions.

Madrid, Spain

The City of Madrid, with a population of about four million, has had an Ombudsman since 1996. The office has 13 staff and costs about £630,000 a year. The Madrid City Parliament decided to establish the office, with the agreement of all political parties, and passed quite detailed legislation. The Ombudsman's general duties are like those of Norway's and Sweden's ombudspeople. The Ombudsman does take on individual cases – 844 in 1998 – as well as representing children as a body. He or she can issue formal recommendations, reminders of legal duties, suggestions and warnings (these have included warning the media over child privacy issues and the portrayal of inaccurate images of children).

The Ombudsman has carried out a systematic programme of visits to residential institutions, daycare centres and so on. Issues worked on by the Ombudsman include: immigrant children living in substandard housing; children and sects; disappeared children; adoption; simulated weapons as toys; children's leisure and free time; a personal identification document for children; identification of newborn babies in hospital; children in hospital; marginalised children generally; a study of children's consumer habits; placing suggestion boxes for children to use in schools and other institutions; development of local children's councils in districts of Madrid with child mayors and town clerks; promotion of a Master's Degree in children's needs and rights at Madrid University.

Effective Government Structures for Children

Summary of a report of a Gulbenkian Foundation Inquiry

Rachel Hodgkin and Peter Newell

The Gulbenkian Foundation set up the Inquiry into Effective Government Structures for Children in 1995, commissioning Rachel Hodgkin and Peter Newell to carry out a wide consultation, and to prepare a report. Sir Peter Newsam chaired an Advisory Group. Questionnaires were circulated throughout the UK, to government departments, governmental bodies, and organisations and individuals in the children's field. Internationally, information was sought on special government structures for children in all countries which have ratified the UN Convention on the Rights of the Child.

There is widespread concern that government structures in the UK are failing children. This report, the result of a wide-ranging inquiry in the UK and internationally, proposes ways of ensuring that central government is more responsive to the needs and rights of children. It aims to move forward the debate on how government should organise itself for children.

The 170-page report first outlines the aims of effective government for children and justifies the case for special structures for children. It goes on to discuss what central government should be doing for children, and to make detailed proposals for alternative structures, both in Whitehall and within Northern Ireland, Scotland and Wales. In addition, it promotes the case for new parliamentary structures, and for an independent Office of Children's Rights Commissioner.

The report is not about the content of policies for children. It is about the structures required to ensure that the process of government meets the needs of children.

Aims of effective government for children

Section 1 of the report sets out the aims of effective government structures:

- to ensure the healthy and happy development of children to their full potential, both as children now, and for the future well-being of our society

- to encourage the active, responsible participation of children in society, enabling them to grow into responsible adults
- to respect and respond to the diversity of children in the UK (including diversity of age, geographical location, cultural and ethnic background, abilities and aspirations)
- to fulfil and develop the spirit as well as the letter of existing domestic children's legislation in all jurisdictions
- to meet international obligations to make children a high political priority, and to implement fully the UN Convention on the Rights of the Child
- to make the best use of inevitably limited resources.

Why government structures for children need changing

Section 2 of the report provides a detailed justification for special government structures for children.

Every citizen deserves sensitive government structures to meet his or her needs. Because government generally is divided by function – education, health, environment and so on – rather than by reference to particular population groups, lack of or inadequate coordination across government is a potential problem for all citizens, not just children. Making the case for a high political priority for children does not diminish the need for appropriate government structures for other defined population groups.

Children justify special structures firstly because their healthy development and active participation are so uniquely crucial to the healthy future of society. In addition:

- Despite their immaturity, children have equal status to adults as members of the human race. They are individuals, not the possessions of parents, nor products of the State, not just people-in-the-making.
- Children's dependence and developmental state makes them particularly vulnerable.
- Children are more affected by the activities – and the inactivities – of government than other age-groups.
- Children lack the vote, or any direct political power, and play no significant part in the political process.
- Current changes in our society – for example to family structures and to employment patterns, and the introduction of market forces to public services – are having a massive impact on children now.
- The financial and social costs of failing to ensure children's healthy development are high. What happens to children in the early years significantly determines their positive or negative development, and their cost or contribution to society over the rest of their lives.
- There is a widespread belief outside government (also acknowledged quite widely within government) that current government structures are failing children.

The report refers to the proliferation of papers, reports and books documenting ways in which government is failing UK children; responses to the Inquiry provided further examples. They are analysed under the following headings:

1 **A failure to give children political priority** The lack of an overt political commitment to children.

2 **The invisibility of children** There is no annual report on the state of UK children, no systematic collection or publication of statistics, no requirement to assess and publish information on the impact of government policies on children and no analysis of budgets to assess the amount and proportion spent on children.

3 **Inadequate coordination between government departments, and between Whitehall and government departments in Northern Ireland, Scotland and Wales** Respondents to the Inquiry singled out many serious problems relating to poor inter-departmental coordination.

4 **The inefficient use of resources in central government** With some exceptions, current structures inhibit flexibility in funding, at central and local levels.

5 **Failure to promote children's responsible participation in society** The report cites the strong evidence that children's and young people's alienation from politics and the democratic process is growing. While there are encouraging developments, there are as yet no consistent government strategies or structures to promote children's active participation in society.

Why not simply improve existing structures?

Some who acknowledge failures in existing structures argue that all that is needed is to recognise the importance of children, and use existing structures and opportunities for coordination. But the report contends that developing a children's perspective, and ensuring that the impact of policies on children is appropriately considered throughout government, demands additional structures, as well as a new political will.

What the report is asking of central government, central government has already begun to demand of local government, through the process of children's services planning.

Why not have special governmental structures for 'families', or 'youth'?

The birth- to 17 year olds are a distinct group with a common set of needs arising from their state of dependency, evolving capacities and disenfranchisement. There is of course concurrence of interests with 'families' and with 'youth', but the definitions are often so wide as to be meaningless, and children's concerns are often eclipsed by those of parents or young adults. The purpose of a focus on children is not to downgrade the importance of adult family members or young adults, but to develop structures to ensure that relevant aspects of family and youth policies are sensitive to children.

International recognition of the need for special structures for children

The report outlines government obligations under the UN Convention. In order to achieve many of the Convention's goals changes to traditional structures are needed, which have been identified by the international monitoring Committee on the Rights of the Child. Similarly, proposals for change have been made in the European Strategy for Children, adopted in 1996.

What government should be doing for children

Section 3 sets out the major functions of effective government for children, reflecting the aims and needs described in Sections 1 and 2.

1 **A Governmental Strategy for UK Children**, providing an over-arching context for development and coordination of policy in England, Northern Ireland, Scotland and Wales needs to be developed and adopted at the heart of government, under the leadership of the Prime Minister and with the authority of the full Cabinet. The Strategy would not be a detailed action plan; such plans, appropriate to the needs of children in England, Northern Ireland, Scotland and Wales and to regions and localities, should be drawn up within its framework. It would provide the overall aims and objectives within which departmental aims and programmes for children would be drafted, and against which they would be evaluated.

 The key foundation for the Strategy would be the UN Convention on the Rights of the Child, already promoted by the Government as the foundation for local strategic planning. Other foundations exist in the first serious attempts at unified children's legislation: the Children Act 1989, Children (Scotland) Act 1995 and the Children (NI) Order 1995, and in the Citizen's Charter principles of public service – as yet little developed for children as citizens.

2 **Making children visible in government** Children's interests are all too often neither seen nor heard in government policy-making and policy review. The report suggests various strategies for developing children's visibility in government processes:

 Child impact analysis: the concept of child impact statements has been little explored in practice. All sectors and levels of government need to assess the impact, both direct and indirect, of existing and proposed legislation and policies on children. The Governmental Strategy for UK Children should provide the basic framework for this assessment. There has been more progress, in the UK and internationally, in requiring assessment of the impact of proposed policies on the environment. The parallels between children and the environment are obvious: both are about the future fate of the country and the planet. It is clear that as with environmental impact, the process of assessing child impact should be built into government.

 Consultation, pilot projects, monitoring, research and evaluation: policies for children should be developed on a sound foundation which incorporates all these processes.

 Budget analysis: there should be sufficient analysis of departmental and other governmental budgets to ensure that the proportion of money being spent on children is identified. Children need to be visible in budgets and financial decision-making. The report points to recent developments in Scandinavian countries where a 'children's annex' to the national budget is published, explaining and costing policies which affect children.

An annual report on 'The State of UK Children': policy development and monitoring implementation of policy within the proposed overall Governmental Strategy for UK Children demands the systematic collection and appropriate dissemination of statistics and other information. A report on 'The State of UK Children' should be prepared annually and presented to Parliament. Distinct reports would be needed for England, Northern Ireland, Scotland and Wales, but they should share the same framework to enable useful comparisons to be made. The report emphasises that giving government the function of annually reporting on children does not remove the need for independent reporting, from the proposed independent children's commissioner and from NGOs.

3 Coordination of government for children Section 2 of the report summarises the widely-expressed concerns about failures of coordination on children's issues throughout government. The need to improve is already recognised; the report outlines current formal and ad hoc arrangements, and makes proposals:

Coordination of central government departments: There should be a Standing Inter-ministerial Group on Children, or a Cabinet Committee or Sub-committee on Children, with a shadow group of senior officials from the relevant government departments.

Reallocating or changing specific departmental responsibilities: There is a case for reviewing particular responsibilities of functional departments – e.g. considering early years care and education, child protection, play and young offenders.

Coordination between central and local government: Local Children's Services Plans should be developed into genuinely cross-sectoral initiatives for all children. This implies central government structures and legislation which enable the key local agencies to take joint responsibility for the plans.

4 Promoting children's active participation in society Central government should take comprehensive legislative and other appropriate steps to recognise children as active participants in society, whose views should be heard and taken seriously in decision-making. The report notes that the principles behind this recommendation are generally accepted: what is needed is universal implementation. In addition, children and their families should have ready access to information about policy development and new legislation affecting them.

Children's and young people's involvement in politics: Lowering the voting age to 16, with a corresponding lowering of the age at which young people can stand for election, should be given serious consideration, together with other strategies for encouraging children's and young people's active engagement in the democratic process.

Proposals for government structures

Section 4 of the report summarises proposals for new government structures, including sections on Northern Ireland, Scotland and Wales (contributed by Paula Rodgers, Kathleen Marshall and Catriona Williams).

The proposals in this section are intended to provoke and inform a more detailed debate on effective government for children. Specific proposals are made, but the report recognises the need to look for pragmatic ways of developing existing structures (for example accepting that at the moment a Cabinet minister whose only responsibility is for children is unlikely to be appointed, although the case for one is fully justified). In addition, arrangements for children will have to be integrated into the overall structure of government, including arrangements for other priority groups and issues, for cross-departmental coordination and for constitutional issues including the consequences of devolution in Northern Ireland, Scotland and Wales.

The report emphasises that without commitment from the highest level – including the support of the Prime Minister of the day – new structures are unlikely to have real impact. A large majority of respondents to the Inquiry favoured the appointment of a Minister for Children, but almost all raised reservations. There is a risk that a weak post could marginalise rather than promote children as a particular priority, or allow some departments to abdicate their responsibilities for children. Both of these dangers are more likely to occur if a Minister for Children is sited in one of the functional departments, or if 'children' is part of a wider ministerial brief. The report suggests that establishing a comprehensive 'Children's Department' is not a feasible proposition at the present time, but that there should be a detailed study of the various ways of creating such a department, reviewing models in other countries. It emphasises the disadvantages of positioning a cross-departmental minister in any one of the functional departments – Health, Education, Home Office and so on. It also reviews the idea of a peripatetic minister for children, able to move into different departments on short-term projects, and the interesting development in Ireland, where the 'Minister for Children' has staffed offices in the Departments of Health, Education and Justice.

The report summarises current government structures affecting children in Northern Ireland, Scotland and Wales, and discusses plans for devolution and their implications for children.

A children's perspective at the heart of government

Within the Prime Minister's Office: appropriate advisers with acknowledged expertise on children.

In Cabinet: a senior Cabinet minister with responsibility for children (probably with other cross-departmental responsibilities). This could be a Deputy Prime Minister, or one of the traditional non-departmental Cabinet posts – Lord President of the Council, Chancellor of the Duchy of Lancaster and so on. Within current constitutional arrangements, the Secretaries of State for Northern Ireland, Scotland and Wales would add the perspective of Northern Ireland, Scottish and Welsh children to Cabinet deliberations.

A minister of state, designated Minister for Children, sited in the Cabinet Office and having direct responsibility for a Cabinet Office Children's Unit. This small unit should come within the Cabinet Office's Domestic Directorate and be headed by a senior civil servant reporting to the Cabinet Secretary (the Unit could have seconded staff from other departments and specialist advisers, and could set up advisory groups to support its work).

Junior ministers with responsibility for children in the Northern Ireland, Scottish and Welsh Offices, reporting to the Secretaries of State. A designated senior civil servant with wide knowledge of children's issues in each Office to ensure coordination between the various departments.

A Cabinet Committee or Sub-committee for Children, or Standing Inter-ministerial Group on Children, with a 'shadow' group of senior officials to oversee the development, implementation and monitoring of the Governmental Strategy for UK Children.

In Parliament

There should be a 'special focus' Select Committee on Children in the House of Commons. The report commends the proposal currently (1996) under consideration for a Select Committee on the Needs of Children and their Families in the House of Lords. The All-Party Parliamentary Groups for Children should become yet more active and link their agendas and activities to the Governmental Strategy for UK Children.

The independent Office of Children's Rights Commissioner

The report commends the detailed proposal presented in another Gulbenkian Foundation report, *Taking Children Seriously*, for a statutory, independent Office of Children's Rights Commissioner, with separate but linked commissioners for England, Northern Ireland, Scotland and Wales. It emphasises that the proposal, now supported by all major children's organisations in the UK, is entirely complementary to proposals for effective structures within government.

Powers and duties of a Minister for Children

The Minister for Children, supported by the Cabinet Office Children's Unit, should have specific powers and duties which could include, in collaboration with equivalent nominated Ministers in Scotland, Wales and Northern Ireland where UK-wide policies are involved, or directly on behalf of children in England:

- drawing up the Governmental Strategy for UK Children, for approval by the Cabinet
- servicing the Cabinet Committee or Sub-committee on Children, or Standing Inter-ministerial Committee on Children, and any other coordinating Sub-committees or ad hoc groups on specific issues, and securing other forms of inter-departmental coordination
- analysing the impact of government policy on children
- reporting annually to Parliament on the current state of children in the UK and on progress towards the objectives identified in the Strategy for Children
- encouraging and facilitating integrated funding between departments and agencies to secure particular outcomes for children (perhaps with a small budget to provide incentives). The Unit would not, however, normally, have a large spending budget – responsibility for public funds would remain with the functional departments
- taking on responsibility for over-arching legislation relating to children
- developing pilot mechanisms for listening and responding to the concerns of

children and young people and stratagies for giving them greater civic responsibilities
- proposing the transfer of, or changes to, specified responsibilities for children
  between departments, and identifying and initiating new mechanisms for
  securing joint responsibility in certain areas
- overseeing and developing joint planning for children's services at a local
  level.

The report indicates that these functions could arguably be achieved through
structural changes and without a Minister for Children, but that this would be
likely to give them a lower status and limit their impact.

Worldwide progress

Section 6 of the report summarises selected responses from more than 60 countries to the Inquiry's international questionnaire, to illustrate the extent to which
countries in all continents have adopted special arrangements intended to make
government more sensitive to children and aid implementation of the UN
Convention.

Appendices to the report present the inter-departmental response to the
Inquiry collated by the Department of Health, on current central government
structures for children, give the text of the Inquiry's questionnaires and list those
who responded to the questionnaires.

The report *Effective Government Structures for Children* is available from:
Turnaround Publisher Services Ltd,
Unit 3, Olympia Trading Estate, Coburg Road, Wood Green, London N22 6TZ
Tel: 020 8829 3000 Fax: 020 8881 5088
Price £10.95, plus £2 p&p
ISBN 0 903319 77 2

Further copies of this summary are available free from:
The Gulbenkian Foundation, 98 Portland Place, London W1N 4ET
Tel: 020 7636 5313 Fax: 020 7637 3421

Principles relating to the status of independent national human rights institutions – the 'Paris Principles'

Following discussion and debate by United Nations agencies and non-governmental organisations concerning the need for national human rights institutions, the 'Principles relating to the Status of National Institutions' (known as the Paris Principles) were adopted by the UN General Assembly in 1993.

This is the text of the Principles:

Competence and responsibilities

1 A national institution shall be vested with competence to promote and protect human rights.

2 A national institution shall be given as broad a mandate as possible, which shall be clearly set forth in a constitutional or legislative text, specifying its composition and its sphere of competence.

3 A national institution shall, inter alia, have the following responsibilities:

(a) To submit to the Government, Parliament and any other competent body, on an advisory basis either at the request of the authorities concerned or through the exercise of its power to hear a matter without higher referral, opinions, recommendations, proposals and reports on any matters concerning the promotion and protection of human rights; the national institution may decide to publicise them; these opinions, recommendations, proposals and reports, as well as any prerogative of the national institution, shall relate to the following areas:

(i) Any legislative or administrative provisions, as well as provisions relating to judicial organisation, intended to preserve and extend the protection of human rights; in that connection, the national institution shall examine the legislation and administrative provisions in force, as well as bills and proposals, and shall make such recommendations as it deems appropriate in order to ensure that these provisions conform to the fundamental principles of human rights; it shall, if necessary, recommend the adoption of new legislation, the amendment of legislation in force and the adoption or amendment of administrative measures.

(ii) Any situation of violation of human rights which it decides to take up.

(iii) The preparation of reports on the national situation with regard to human rights in general, and on more specific matters.

(iv) Drawing the attention of the Government to situations in any part of the country where human rights are violated and making proposals to it for initiatives to put an end to such situations and, where necessary, expressing an opinion on the positions and reactions of the Government.

(b) To promote and ensure the harmonisation of national legislation, regulations and practices with the international human rights instruments to which the State is a party, and their effective implementation.

(c) To encourage ratification of the above-mentioned instruments or accession to those instruments, and to ensure their implementation.

(d) To contribute to the reports which States are required to submit to United Nations bodies and committees, and to regional institutions, pursuant to their treaty obligations, and, where necessary, to express an opinion on the subject, with due respect for their independence.

(e) To cooperate with the United Nations and any other organisation in the United Nations system, the regional institutions and the national institutions of other countries that are competent in the areas of the promotion and protection of human rights.

(f) To assist in the formulation of programmes for the teaching of, and research into, human rights and to take part in their execution in schools, universities and professional circles.

(g) To publicise human rights and efforts to combat all forms of discrimination, in particular racial discrimination, by increasing public awareness; especially through information and education and by making use of all press organs.

Composition and guarantees of independence and pluralism

1 The composition of the national institution and the appointment of its members, whether by means of an election or otherwise, shall be established in accordance with a procedure which affords all necessary guarantees to ensure the pluralist representation of the social forces (of civilian society) involved in the promotion and protection of human rights, particularly by powers which will enable effective cooperation to be established with, or through the presence of, representatives of:

(a) Non-governmental organisations responsible for human rights and efforts to combat racial discrimination, trade unions, concerned social and professional organisations, for example, associations of lawyers, doctors, journalists and eminent scientists.

(b) Trends in philosophical or religious thought

(c) Universities and qualified experts

(d) Parliament

(e) Government departments (if they are included, these representatives should participate in the deliberations only in an advisory capacity).

2 The national institution shall have an infrastructure which is suited to the smooth conduct of its activities, in particular adequate funding. The purpose of this funding should be to enable it to have its own staff and premises, in order to be independent of the Government and not to be subject to financial control which might affect its independence.

3 In order to ensure a stable mandate for the members of the institution, without which there can be no real independence, their appointment shall be effected by an official act which shall establish the specific duration of the mandate. This mandate may be renewable, provided that the pluralism of the institution's membership is ensured.

Methods of operation

Within the framework of its operation, the national institution shall:

(a) Freely consider any questions falling within its competence, whether they are submitted by the Government or taken up by it without referral to a higher authority, on the proposal of its members or of any petitioner.

(b) Hear any person and obtain any information and any documents necessary for assessing situations falling within its competence.

(c) Address public opinion directly or through any press organ, particularly in order to publicise its opinions and recommendations.

(d) Meet on a regular basis and whenever necessary in the presence of all its members after they have been duly convened.

(e) Establish working groups from among its members as necessary, and set up local or regional sections to assist it in discharging its functions.

(f) Maintain consultation with the other bodies, whether jurisdictional or other-wise, responsible for the promotion and protection of human rights (in particular, ombudsmen, mediators and similar institutions).

(g) In view of the fundamental role played by non-governmental organisations in expanding the work of national institutions, develop relations with non-governmental organisations devoted to promoting and protecting human rights, to economic and social development, to combating racism, to protecting particularly vulnerable groups (especially children, migrant workers, refugees, physically and mentally disabled persons) or to specialised areas.

Additional principles concerning the status of commissions with quasi-jurisdictional competence

A national institution may be authorised to hear and consider complaints and petitions concerning individual situations. Cases may be brought before it by individuals, their representatives, third parties, non-governmental organisations, associations of trade unions or any other representative organisations. In such circumstances, and without prejudice to the principles stated above concerning the other powers of the commissions, the functions entrusted to them may be based on the following principles:

(a) Seeking an amicable settlement through conciliation or, within the limits prescribed by the law, through binding decisions or, where necessary, on the basis of confidentiality.

(b) Informing the party who filed the petition of his rights, in particular the remedies available to him, and promoting his access to them.

(c) Hearing any complaints or petitions or transmitting them to any other competent authority within the limits prescribed by the law.

(d) Making recommendations to the competent authorities, especially by proposing amendments or reforms of the laws, regulations and administrative practices, especially if they have created the difficulties encountered by the persons filing the petitions in order to assert their rights.

Examples of laws establishing independent offices for children in Europe

Norway

Norway's original Act and Standing Instructions were adopted in 1981. They were most recently amended in 1998.

Act no. 5 of 6 March 1981 relating to the Ombudsman for Children (as amended 17 July 1998)

1 Purpose
The purpose of this Act is to contribute to promoting the interests of children in society.

2 Ombudsman for Children
The King shall appoint an Ombudsman for Children for a period of four years.

3 Duties of the Ombudsman
The duties of the Ombudsman are to promote the interests of children vis-à-vis public and private authorities and to follow up the development of conditions under which children grow up.

In particular the Ombudsman shall:

- on his own initiative or through consultation protect the interests of children in connection with planning and study-reports in all fields
- ensure that legislation relating to the protection of children's interests is observed, including whether Norwegian law and administrative routines are in accordance with Norway's obligations under the UN Convention on the Rights of the Child
- propose measures which can strengthen children's safety under the law
- put forward proposals for measures which can solve or prevent conflicts between children and society
- ensure that sufficient information is given to the public and private sectors concerning children's rights and measures required for children.

The Ombudsman may act on his own initiative or at the request of other people. The Ombudsman for Children himself decides whether an application offers sufficient grounds for action.

4 Access to institutions and duty to provide information, etc.

The Ombudsman shall have free access to all public and private institutions for children.

Government authorities and public and private institutions for children shall, notwithstanding the pledge of secrecy, give the Ombudsman the information needed to carry out the duties of the Ombudsman pursuant to this Act. Information which is needed for the accomplishment of the Ombudsman's tasks pursuant to clause 3, second paragraph, may also, notwithstanding the pledge of secrecy, be demanded from others. When information can be demanded pursuant to this item, it may also be required that records and other documents be produced.

The rules laid down in subsections 1, 204 and 205–209 of the Civil Disputes Act are correspondingly applicable to the Ombudsman's right to demand information. Disputes as to the application of these rules may be brought before the District and City Courts, which shall decide the question by a court ruling.

5 Statements from the Ombudsman

The Ombudsman has the right to make statements concerning conditions included in his working sphere, according to this Act and the Instructions for the Ombudsman. The Ombudsman himself decides to whom these statements shall be directed.

6 Instructions for the Ombudsman

The King lays down general instructions for the organisation and procedures of the Ombudsman. Beyond this the Ombudsman carries out his functions independently.

7 Entry into force, etc.

This Act is also applicable to Svalbard.

The Act shall enter into force from the date prescribed by the King.

Instructions for the Ombudsman for Children

Laid down by Royal Decree of 11 September 1981 with amendments including the latest by Royal Decree of 17 July 1998

1 Duties

In accordance with these instructions the Ombudsman for Children shall carry out the duties of the office according to the Act relating to the Ombudsman for Children. The Ombudsman in pursuing his duties shall work to ensure that the needs, rights and interests of children are given the necessary consideration in all areas of society. The Ombudsman does not have the authority to decide cases or set aside decisions in the administration. The term 'children' shall here be understood to mean persons up to the age of majority.

The Ombudsman should ensure that the public is informed about his work.

2 How cases are taken up

The Ombudsman takes up cases on his own initiative or at the request of other people.

Anyone may apply to the Ombudsman. The Ombudsman shall ensure that verbal applications are put into writing.

A person applying to the Ombudsman should, in so far as possible, explain the grounds for the application and submit whatever information and documents are available in this case.

If an application concerns a specific child and the application does not come from the child itself, the Ombudsman shall not deal with the case without the permission of the relevant child. When the child's age so indicates, the permission of the guardian shall also be obtained. If general considerations so indicate, the Ombudsman may deal with the case even though permission as mentioned above has not been obtained.

3 Rejection

The Ombudsman shall reject applications concerning specific, individual conflicts between a child and its guardians, and between the guardians mutually concerning the exercise of parental responsibility and similar matters. The Ombudsman shall also reject applications that partly cover such conflicts, unless the Ombudsman, after a concrete assessment, finds that the interests of the child will obviously be neglected through this rejection.

The Ombudsman shall in such cases give the reason for the rejection and offer information about any existing instances established for the purpose of handling conflicts of this nature.

A rejection by the Ombudsman cannot be appealed.

4 Referrals

Applications relating to conditions which in the main concern questions relating to the application of the law or the handling of the case are to be referred by the Ombudsman to the Storting's Ombudsman for Public Administration when this is relevant.

If an application concerns a situation which may be brought before an administrative agency, the person applying to the Ombudsman for Children shall be advised to take the matter up with the relevant body. The Ombudsman himself may also send the matter to this body.

If an application concerns a situation which can be referred to the Public Prosecution Authority or a special supervisory body, after a more detailed investigation of the circumstances of the case the Ombudsman may send the case to the relevant authority if the conditions pursuant to subsection 6 of clause 13b of the Public Administration Act obtain.

5 Shelving of cases

If the Ombudsman finds that application has been made concerning a situation which does not offer grounds for criticism or for any other follow-up procedure, the case may be shelved. The Ombudsman may also shelve a case if the situation which the application concerns has been remedied or has ceased to exist.

At any stage in the proceedings, the Ombudsman may also shelve a case for reasons of pressure of work. However, the Ombudsman should try to deal with a representative selection of cases.

Anyone who has applied to the Ombudsman shall be informed of the shelving of the case and the reason for this.

The shelving of the case by the Ombudsman cannot be appealed.

6 Rules for dealing with cases

Chapters I–III of the Public Administration Act and the Freedom of Information Act are applicable to the activity of the Ombudsman.

Before making his statement the Ombudsman shall ensure that the case is clarified as far as possible. The Ombudsman determines what steps should be taken to clarify the circumstances in the case.

Also when this does not follow from other rules the Ombudsman shall preserve secrecy about the source of information he has used when the source has expressly requested this, or if the Ombudsman finds this appropriate on behalf of the child.

7 The Ombudsman's statement on the case

The Ombudsman shall personally adopt a standpoint on all cases that have been taken up for discussion and have not been shelved pursuant to clause 5 of the Instructions. As a basic rule the opinion of the Ombudsman shall be formulated as a written statement, giving the grounds for this.

The Ombudsman himself decides to whom the statement shall be directed. The statement can also be directed to the press and the broadcasting corporation or others to the extent that the Ombudsman finds expedient.

The Ombudsman shall not express an opinion on the position in regard to the law when the Storting's Ombudsman for Public Administration has made a statement or when the situation has either been decided by the courts or has been brought before the courts for a decision. Neither shall the Ombudsman express an opinion in cases that are under police investigation and where children might have been exposed to acts in violation of the law, insofar as somebody is under suspicion or indicted in the case. Even so, the Ombudsman may criticise the factual and legal situation which has been revealed by the Ombudsman for Public Administration's statement, by the police investigation or by the decision of the courts.

8 Annual Report

Each year by 1 April the Ombudsman shall submit a report to the Ministry about his activities in the preceding calendar year.

The report shall be available to the public.

9 Personnel and financial administration

The Ombudsman is appointed by the Council of State for a period of four years. No one can be Ombudsman for more than a total of eight years.

The Ombudsman has a secretariat available to him to assist with his work. The staff of the secretariat are employed according to rules laid down by the Ministry.

The Ombudsman himself appoints one of the staff as permanent deputy for the Ombudsman. The Ombudsman and his Executive Officers should have varied professional backgrounds.

The rules for the administration of the finances in the Ministries and the rules for the organisation and work procedures of the Ministries shall be applicable insofar as possible.

10 The Advisory Board for the Ombudsman for Children
Cancelled by Royal Decree of 17 July 1998.

11 Entry into force
These instructions enter into force 1 September 1998.

Norwegian Children's Ombudsman,
Barneombudet, PO Box 8036 DEP, N-0030 Oslo, Norway
Tel: 00 47 22 242 630 Fax: 0047 22 249 524

Sweden

In Sweden a short two-section Act to establish the Office of Children's Ombudsman was adopted in 1993. Standing Instructions expand on the role of the Ombudsman:

Act to establish the Office of the Children's Ombudsman

1 The Children's Ombudsman has the task of observing matters relating to the rights and interests of children and young persons. In particular the Ombudsman shall observe the compliance of Acts of the Riksdag, other statutory instruments and implementation of the same with Sweden's commitments under the United Nations Convention on the Rights of the Child.
2 The Children's Ombudsman is assisted by a special Council. The Ombudsman is Chairman of the Council and directs its activities. The Ombudsman and other members of the Council are appointed by the Government for a specified period.
   The Act enters into force on 1 July 1993.

Standing instructions:

Within the scope of its responsibilities, the Office of the Children's Ombudsman shall:
1 initiate measures for asserting the rights and interests of children and young persons
2 represent and support children and young persons in public debate
3 propose to the Government the legislative changes or other measures needed in order for the rights and interests of children and young people to be provided for and
4 initiate the coordination of public measures of prevention in the context of child safety.
The Office of the Children's Ombudsman shall devote special attention to questions relating to children and young people at risk.

The Office of the Children's Ombudsman shall in the course of its activities maintain contacts with children and young persons and with voluntary organisations, public authorities etc., and shall actively observe research and development work relating to children and young persons.

The Office of the Children's Ombudsman shall, not later than 1 October every year, present to the Government a report on its activities between 1 July of the preceding year and 30 June of the current year.

Office of the Children's Ombudsman,
Box 22106, S-10422 Stockholm, Sweden
Tel: 00 46 8 692 2950 Fax: 00 46 8 654 6277
Website: www.bo.se

Denmark

The Danish National Council for Children was established for a three-year trial period in 1994. Following an evaluation of its first three years' work, in 1997 the Council was established as a permanent body through legislation.

Order establishing Denmark's National Council for Children
Ministry of Social Affairs, Order no. 2 of 5 January 1998

In pursuance of section 88 of Act no. 453 of 10 June 1997 on the rule of law and administration in social areas, the following provisions shall be laid down:

1 The Minister of Social Affairs establishes a National Council for Children which shall work on ensuring children's rights and focusing on and providing information about children's conditions in society. The Council shall advise authorities on matters relating to children's conditions and include children's points of view in its work.

   Moreover, the Council shall assess the conditions under which children in Denmark live, in the light of the provisions and intentions set out in the United Nations Convention on the Rights of the Child.

2 (1) The Council shall be independent and interdisciplinary. Together the members shall represent insight into a wide spectrum of issues concerning children's upbringing and development, children's schooling, cultural and leisure life, children's health, children's legal status and children with special needs.

   (2) The Council shall be made up of one chairman and six members. The Minister of Social Affairs shall appoint the chairman and two members as well as two alternates. Four members and four alternates shall be appointed on the recommendation of an electoral assembly made up of organisations working in the children's field.

   (3) The chairman and the other members of the Council shall function for a term of four years from 1 July. On their first appointment as at 1 July 1998, the term of their office shall be two years for members and alternates appointed by the Minister of Social Affairs.

Members continue until new members have been appointed. Members may only be eligible for one re-appointment.

(4) The National Council for Children shall elect a deputy chairman from among its members. The deputy chairman shall deputise for the Chairman.

(5) Alternates shall attend Council meetings on behalf of members in the event of long-term absence.

(6) Alternates shall replace for the unexpired term of the original appointment of any member who retires from the National Council for Children.

3   A permanent secretariat shall be attached to the National Council for Children.

4   (1) The National Council for Children shall hold an annual meeting with the organisations and associations making up the electoral assembly and with authorities etc. with responsibilities in the field of children.

(2) Every year the National Council for Children shall make a report in writing on the activities of the Council which shall be distributed to the circle of people referred to in subsection (1).

5   The National Council for Children shall lay down its own rules of procedure. The Minister of Social Affairs shall approve the rules of procedure.

6   (1) The National Council for Children shall:

   (i) assess and identify conditions in the development of society in general which may possibly have an adverse impact on children's opportunities to develop;

   (ii) follow and render visible developments in the conditions of children's upbringing, and moreover identify matters in legislation and administrative practice where children's needs and rights are not met sufficiently or are directly ignored or which are inappropriate in the light of the safeguarding of a good childhood and adolescence;

   (iii) pass on information about children, bring topical issues up for debate and plead the cause of children in the public debate; and

   (iv) work to give children better opportunities of participating in the debate and influencing developments in society.

(2) Moreover, the National Council for Children is allowed to take up general issues and request public authorities to account for political decisions and administrative practice relating to those issues.

(3) In connection with the legislative initiatives and other initiatives which are important to children's upbringing, the National Council for Children will be heard.

(4) The National Council for Children cannot take up specific complaints for consideration.

7   The National Council for Children may itself take initiatives and make proposals for alterations in the areas referred to in section 6 (1) and (2) above.

8   The Folketing (the Danish Parliament), ministers and national authorities may consult the National Council for Children in all matters of a general nature which are important to the conditions of children in society, for example to ensure that children's rights, needs and interests are safeguarded in social planning.

9   The Council may involve special experts in its work.

10   (1) Organisations, associations, etc., working in the field of the upbringing of

children, shall appoint one member to the electoral assembly referred to under section 2 (2) above.

(2) Each member of the electoral assembly shall have a vote and the right to offer himself or herself as a candidate for the National Council for Children.

(3) The electoral assembly shall be convened at the annual meeting referred to under section 4 (1) above.

(4) The Ministry of Social Affairs shall decide finally which new organisations, associations, etc., may be represented in the electoral assembly.

11 Funds for the activities of the Council will be voted in the annual Finance Acts.

12 This Order shall come into force on 1 July 1998.

Minister of Social Affairs, 5 January 1998

Karen Jespersen / Anders Lynge Madsen

Børnerådet – National Council for Children, Denmark
Holmens Kanal 22, 1060 Copenhagen, Denmark
Tel: 00 45 3392 4500 Fax: 00 45 3392 4699
E-mail: brd@sm.dk Website: www.boerneraadet.dk

Belgium – Flemish Community

In 1997 the Flemish Parliament in Belgium adopted a decree to establish a Commission for Children's Rights and a Commissioner. The Commissioner was appointed in 1998.

Text of the decree passed on 15 July 1997:

Art. 1 The present decree concerns a regional and community matter.

Art. 2 For the purpose of the present decree:

(1) 'Convention' means the Convention on the Rights of the Child, adopted in New York on 20 November 1989.

(2) 'Commission for Children's Rights' means the Commissioner for Children's Rights and the staff who assist him or her in carrying out his or her duties.

(3) 'Child' means any minor.

(4) 'Administrative authority' means administrative authority in the sense of the joint legislation of the Council of State, dealing with the powers of the Flemish Community and the Flemish Region.

(5) 'Institutions' means all private institutions recognised by the Flemish Government or by Flemish public bodies.

Art. 3

(1) The post of Commissioner for Children's Rights, hereinafter called 'the Commissioner', is hereby established.

(2) The Commissioner shall be appointed by the Flemish Parliament.

(3) The conditions of employment of the staff of the Commission for Children's Rights shall be determined by the Flemish Parliament on the proposal of the Commissioner.

Art. 4 The Commissioner shall defend the rights and interests of the child.

To this end he or she shall:

(1) monitor respect for the Convention

(2) ensure the monitoring, analysis and assessment of children's conditions of life

(3) act as the defender of children's rights, interests and needs.

Art. 5 In execution of the duties laid down in Art. 4, the Commissioner, having regard to the Convention, shall ensure in particular:

(1) dialogue with children and with organisations active in the field of individual and collective services to children or in the defence of children's interests

(2) the social participation of children and the accessibility to children of all services and organisations of interest to them

(3) the monitoring of the conformity to the Convention of all laws, decrees, ordinances and other legislative instruments, including procedural regulations governing any matter which falls within the jurisdiction of the Flemish community or the Flemish region

(4) the dissemination of information relating to the content of the Convention, especially in the interests of children.

To this end, the Commissioner may call in particular upon the experience and scientific experience of the *Vlaams Centrum voor de Bevordering van het Welzijn van Kinderen en Gezinnen* (the Flemish Centre for the Promotion of Child and Family Welfare), without however in any case hindering the activities of the Centre.

Art. 6 In the fulfilment of the duties laid down in Art. 4 the Commissioner shall be empowered:

(1) to carry out investigations on his or her own initiative or on the request of the Flemish Parliament into any matter relating to respect for the Convention

(2) to examine any complaint regarding non-respect of the Convention, and as far as is possible to refer it to the [relevant] institutions. The examination of a complaint shall be suspended in the case of legal proceedings or administrative appeal in the matter of the complaint. The administrative authority shall notify the Commissioner of any appeal lodged. The making of a complaint and its examination shall in no way affect the time-limits for appeals in the courts or in the administrative tribunals. The Commissioner shall inform the complainant of the outcome of the complaint.

Art. 7

(1) At his or her appointment and during his or her period in post the Commissioner shall satisfy the following conditions:

(i) have Belgian nationality, be resident in the Flemish region or in a bilingual area of metropolitan Brussels, and be the holder of a Flemish-speaking certificate

(ii) be of irreproachable conduct

(iii) enjoy full civil and political rights

(iv) hold a university degree or equivalent

(v) have at least 5 years' professional experience relevant to the post

(iv) correspond to the profile determined by the Flemish Parliament.

(2) The Flemish Parliament shall appoint the Commissioner for a term of 5 years, which may be extended once.

(3) Before entering into post, the Commissioner shall take the following oath before the President of the Flemish Parliament:

'I swear to be faithful to the King of the Belgians, to obey the Constitution and the laws of the Belgian people.'

Art. 8

(1) Appointment to the post of Commissioner is not compatible with the holding of any other mandate, post or position, paid or unpaid.

The Commissioner shall not have held public electoral office in the three years before appointment.

During the three years following the termination of the appointment the Commissioner shall not be nominated as a candidate for public electoral office. For the purposes of the present paragraph, the posts of burgomaster appointed from without the municipal council, of administrator of a public body, and appointments as a government commissioner or governor, deputy governor or vice-governor shall be regarded as equivalent to electoral office.

(2) The Commissioner shall enjoy the status of a councillor of the *Cour des Comptes.*

The rules governing the payment of councillors of the *Cour des Comptes*, included in the law of 21 March 1964 on the payment of members of the *Cour des Comptes,* shall apply to the Commissioner.

(3) Within the limits of his or her own competence, the Commissioner shall receive no instruction from any authority. The Commissioner shall be entirely independent in the exercise of his or her functions.

The Commissioner may not be relieved of his or her post by reason of acts carried out in the context of his or her duties.

Art. 9 The Flemish Parliament may terminate the appointment of the Commissioner:

(1) at his or her own request

(2) when he or she reaches the age of 65

(3) in the case of such incompatibility as is referred to in Art. 8.1

(4) for grave cause, without prejudice to Art. 8.3.

Art. 10

(1) The authorities shall make available to the Commissioner all information required for the fulfilment of his or her duties. They shall provide on request all relevant information and documentation.

(2) The Commissioner, in the exercise of his or her duties, may request the opinion of the authorities.

(3) Without prejudice to clause 15 of the Constitution, the Commissioner shall have free access to all public buildings and institutions. Public officers and members of their staff shall be duty bound to communicate to the Commissioner any material or information he or she may consider relevant, except such as may be protected by medical confidentiality or which he or she may have been given in confidence.

Art. 11 Article 485 of the *Code pénal* shall be applicable to the Commissioner and his or her staff.

Art. 12

(1) The Commissioner shall address to the Flemish Parliament an annual report on his or her activities as described in Art. 4.

The report shall be discussed by the Parliament in plenary session. The report shall be made public. The Commissioner may also, should he or she consider it useful, make interim reports to the President of the Flemish Parliament with a view to discussion in plenary session.

(2) The Commissioner shall communicate his or her reports to the federal authorities, so that they may take them into account in drawing up the report which Belgium is required to submit every five years to the Committee on the Rights of the Child, in application of Art. 44 of the Convention. The Commissioner shall evaluate this report.

Art. 13 The Flemish Parliament shall determine annually, on the proposal of the Commissioner, the funds necessary for the operation of the Commission for Children's Rights.

Art. 14 Within 6 months of his or her appointment, the Commissioner shall draw up a proposal for standing orders for the operation of the Commission. Upon approval by the Flemish Parliament these regulations and any amendments to them shall be published in the *Moniteur Belge*.

The present decree is promulgated, and ordered to be published in the *Moniteur Belge*.

Brussels, 15 July 1997.

The Minister-President of the Flemish Government,

L. van den Brande

The Flemish Minister of Culture, the Family and Social Affairs,

L. Martens

Kinderrechtencommissariaat, Vlaams Parlement, 1011 Brussels, Belgium
Tel: 00 32 2 552 9800 Fax: 00 32 2 552 9801
E-mail: kinderrechten@vlaamsparlement.be

Russian Federation

Five of the 89 regions of the Russian Federation – city regions or 'oblasts' – have appointed independent offices for children – children's ombudsmen or commissioners for children's rights. These offices have been initiated through a joint project of the Federal Ministry of Labour and Social Development and UNICEF. The following is the Decree establishing the Office of Ombudsman for Children for the City of Ekaterinburg (population one million):

Provisional Regulations on the Office of the Ombudsman for Children residing in the City of Ekaterinburg

The present Regulations define procedures for appointing the Ombudsman for Children in the City of Ekaterinburg, the Ombudsman's powers, as well as mechanisms and conditions of the Ombudsman's work.

The objectives are:

- To ensure priority of policies concerning children and adolescents.
- To improve sufficiency of implementation of federal, oblast and city laws and regulations.
- To advocate and to increase public awareness of children's rights.

General Provisions

1 (1) The office of Ombudsman for Children is established in compliance with the Constitution of the Russian Federation, Federal legislation of the Russian Federation, the Oblast law 'On Protection of Children's Rights', the City of Ekaterinburg Constitution, and other legal instruments that regulate advocacy of children's rights, as well as with the UN Convention on the Rights of the Child.

(2) The Ombudsman is appointed by the Head of the City of Ekaterinburg and approved by the City Duma. The Ombudsman is a municipal officer and is granted all the legal guarantees.

(3) The institution of the Ombudsman for Children is established in order to guarantee state protection of children's rights, compliance with and respect for these rights by the state and local authorities and officials.

(4) The Ombudsman promotes remedial measures in case of children's rights violation, improvement of existing legislation, compliance with the Oblast law 'On Protection of Children's Rights' and the UN Convention on the Rights of the Child, as well as legal education in matters of children's rights and in norms and procedures for their protection.

(5) In exercising his or her duties, the Ombudsman is independent from and not accountable to any municipal officials of the City.

(6) In exercising his or her duties, the Ombudsman follows the constitution of the Russian Federation, Russian Federation legislation, the Oblast law 'On Protection of Children's Rights', the City constitution, the UN Convention on the Rights of the Child, as well as internationally admitted legal norms and principles and international treaties of which the Russian Federation is a signatory.

(7) The Ombudsman's work complements the existing means of children's rights advocacy, and does not annul or revise the competence of the state authorities who are charged with protection or restitution of children's rights.

(8) The Office of the Ombudsman for Children in the City of Ekaterinburg is established in connection with participation in the pilot project supported by UNICEF and the Ministry of Labour and Social Development of the Russian Federation.

The Ombudsman will be briefed, trained, supplied with relevant literature and provided with international and Russian expertise by the UNICEF mission in the Russian Federation and by the Ministry of Labour and Social Development of the Russian Federation.

Procedures for the Ombudsman's Appointment to and Removal from Office

2 (1) The person eligible for the office of Ombudsman for Children should be a citizen of the Russian Federation, a City of Ekaterinburg resident, at least 35 years of age, knowledgeable in the area of children's rights and experienced in their advocacy.

(2) Nominations for the Ombudsman office are submitted by the Head of the City to the City Duma one month before the end of the current Ombudsman's tenure.

(3) The Ombudsman is appointed to and removed from office by the Head of the City, with approval of the City Duma.

(4) The term of the Ombudsman's appointment is 5 years. The Office is funded from the local budget, with a separate section.

(5) Expiration of the term of the office for the Head of the City and/or for the City Duma does not entail the expiration of the term of the current Ombudsman's office.

(6) The same person may not be appointed to the Ombudsman's office for more than two consecutive terms.

(7) The Ombudsman may not be member-elect of an elected body, nor engage in other paid or unpaid activities, with the exception of teaching, research and other creative work.

(8) The Ombudsman may not engage in politics and/or be a member of a political party.

Safeguards for the Ombudsman's Office

3   (1) The Ombudsman is granted immunity throughout the term of his or her office.

(2) The Ombudsman's immunity extends to his or her workplace and place of residence, personal effects, personal and office vehicles, correspondence, personal communications and documents.

(3) The Ombudsman may be administratively or criminally liable and prosecuted at law, as well as arrested, detained, and subjected to a search, only with the consent of the City Duma, except when caught *in flagrante delicto.*

(4) The Ombudsman may be removed from office prior to the end of his or her term in the following cases:

• violation of provisions in articles 3.5. and 3.6. of the present Regulations
• the Ombudsman's conviction in a court of law.

(5) The Ombudsman may be discharged from office in the event of his or her being incapable (due to state of health or other reasons) to exercise his or her functions over a prolonged period of time (no less than 4 consecutive months).

(6) The Ombudsman may be discharged from office in the event that he or she files his or her resignation.

The Ombudsman's Authority

4   (1) The Ombudsman's authority to advocate children's rights extends to all children and adolescents residing in the City of Ekaterinburg.

A child is defined as a person under the age of majority, i.e. from the moment of birth till 18 years of age.

(2) The Ombudsman safeguards the priority given to children under the social policy of the municipal entity 'The City of Ekaterinburg'.

(3) The Ombudsman's authority extends to:

• advocacy of children's rights and interests protected by the law, including: personal rights, right to live with and be brought up by the family, right to education, right to work, right to rest and leisure, right to freedom of expression, right to preserve identity, right to protection from libel or slander, right to freedom of religion, right to protection of privacy
• advocacy of children's property rights and interests, including: right to

adequate standard of living, right to interest in family estate, right to social support, rights and interests of inheritance

- advocacy of rights and interests of disabled and disadvantaged children, including: right to social support, protection of disabled children's rights, rights of children with limited physical abilities, rights of orphans, abandoned children, children in extreme situations, and juvenile offenders

- representation and advocacy of children's rights and lawful interests jointly with the custody and guardianship offices, courts, prosecutors' offices, notaries' offices, registry offices, juvenile commission, state and municipal child and family welfare services.

(4) The Ombudsman's work is based upon glasnost, openness, and accessibility.

(5) The Ombudsman at his or her own discretion administers complaints about decisions, actions (or inaction) of the local authorities, municipal officers, municipal employees in cases when the complainant has previously appealed against these decisions, actions (or inaction) in court or administratively, but does not agree with the appeal decision.

(6)Implementing his or her authority, the Ombudsman has the right to: unrestricted access to all state and local authorities, right to attend meetings of their collegial bodies, as well as the right to unrestricted access to firms, organisations, offices and institutions, regardless of their legal or ownership status, and to public associations.

(7) All materials received by the Ombudsman in course of processing a complaint shall remain confidential until the final decision is made.

(8) After investigating a complaint, the Ombudsman has the right to take legal action (bring a case to court or prosecutor's office) in order to protect violated rights and liberties of children, as well as to attend and monitor juvenile court proceedings.

(9) Mass media founded (or co-founded) by the local authorities, state-owned enterprises, offices and organisations, as well as mass media entirely or partially funded from the City budget, may not refuse the Ombudsman the right to publish or broadcast his or her documents.

(10) After the end of a calendar year, the Ombudsman submits his or her annual report to the Head of the City, to the City Duma, to the UNICEF mission in Russia, and to the Ministry of Labour and Social Development.

(11) All officials are required to provide the Ombudsman with unimpeded access free of charge to all requested materials, documents and other information necessary for him or her to fulfil the obligations of the office. Documents and materials in custody of these officials must be presented to the Ombudsman no later than 15 days after the request is filed, unless the request specifies another date.

(12) Interference with the Ombudsman's work in order to influence his or her decisions, as well as in order to obstruct the Ombudsman's work, will be prosecuted according to the existing legislation of the Russian Federation.

(13) In order to assist the Ombudsman's office, an advisory body may be established under the auspices of the Head of the City.